Y0-AET-658

Also by George Mazzei

THE NEW OFFICE ETIQUETTE:
A Guide to Getting Along in the Corporate Age

MOVING UP
Digging In, Taking Charge, Playing the Power Game and Learning to Like It

George Mazzei

Poseidon Press
New York

A Poseidon Press Book
Published by Pocket Books
A Division of Simon & Schuster, Inc.
Simon & Schuster Building
Rockefeller Center
1230 Avenue of the Americas
New York, New York 10020

Designed by Irving Perkins Associates
Manufactured in the United States of America
1 2 3 4 5 6 7 8 9 10
Library of Congress Cataloging in Publication Data

Mazzei, George.
Moving up.

Includes index.
1. Executive ability. I. Title.
HD38.2.M39 1984 658.4'09 84-15909
ISBN 0-671-50266-2

DEDICATION

To my mother, my sisters, Delores and Nancy, and my Aunt Luciann, with love and thanks for everything

Acknowledgments

The author wishes to thank these people, as well as the many others who did not want to be mentioned by name, for sharing their wisdom, insights and personal experiences with the readers of this book:

Nancy Breyer, Brian Burdine, Muriel Burns, Steven Byers, Patricia Capon, David Arthur Charleson, Tony Clementi, Ethel Leonara Crisp, Robert Dahlin, James Peter Duncan, Mace Duncan, Martin J. Goff, Charles Hix, Ingrid Jacobsen, Dianne Keogh, Thomas Keywan, Elaine S. Laurence, Ann Patty, Hugh Stanford Porter, Anne Quilles, Maria Rodriguez, Karen Solem, Mary Ann Stuart, Shannon Such, John R. Sullivan, and Raul Tapia.

Contents

Introduction

Getting There

IT IS THE desire of most people in business to move up to the top of the heap. The executive framework is based on the wish of men and women at entry levels and at middle- and upper-management positions to gain the big prize—to be boss of the whole operation. Power. Prestige. Perks. Even the young lad in the mailroom may entertain this dream. Many people still rise from these positions to sales positions, to upper management, to second and even first in command.

Seldom is this fantasy of millions accompanied by any self-evaluation when the prizes start being offered. Does anyone ever ask, Am I truly qualified to lead? Do I really know what the job is all about? Will I really do it as well as I did all the jobs leading up to it? Do I really want to do the job or am I dazzled by the idea of being a star?

Even less often does anyone clawing his or her way to the top take a breather to prepare for the job, educationally or through inquiry, in the event it does happen. The general drill is to accept the job, drink some champagne, then dive in hoping the new secretary knows what to do about those blind areas, those job duties that no one ever told you about. Budgets. Boring breakfasts with the biggies. Requisition forms; personnel forms; Internal Revenue Service forms.

And people. Suddenly your little quirks and notions aren't as cute as they were when you were a bright kid with lots of promise, not to mention pizzazz. Now you may be viewed as a stumbling block to other people's careers, or just someone who is difficult, impulsive or blindly idealistic. Creative types often find themselves in this predicament. You may have excelled as a star copywriter at an ad agency, for instance. Your commercials for antacids are awesomely clever, become widely imitated and enter the American vernacular. The next logical step is to move you out of this creative position into a managerial spot, where you must deal with other creative temperaments, sell clients on ideas, try to set up budgets—budgets!—when you had been only faintly aware that all that stuff cost money. Now you are a diplomat, an arbiter, a salesperson, when all you wanted was to drop stunningly clever copy on the world, take your big bucks and spend three days a week at the Hamptons. That's the American Dream for you.

One of the problems in approaching your career is the constant passage of time. You may see yourself as attaining a position of notability and maintaining it until you decide to retire with honors. The rest of the world sees you as one of a line of moving ducks, such as one finds in a shooting gallery. In front of you are people who have occupied your positions before you; tailing you are new bright young people looking to occupy yours. Your survival depends on your ability to continue making the run through the years without being picked off. If you've never wondered what happens to all the bright young people when they get older and their numbers don't match the fewer and fewer upper-level positions, here is your opportunity to do so.

Of course people die along the way, which accounts for a percentage. But where are the others who did not move up, did not become bosses, who were replaced by newer talents? Did they fall victim to midlife crises? Were they used for experiments by aliens from outer space? Primarily, the people who remain on the corporate scene are those who have developed the abilities to survive, learned how the system works, and looked ahead at each step of the way to see what they were getting themselves into and how they could work it to their own advantage. There are three basic areas which need to be dealt with in detail for such survival: personal interaction; diplomacy and power; and the mechanics of being boss. All in all, the business of doing business.

Yes, it is necessary to work your way to the top, but your interpretation of what "work" means in this context becomes important. I had a very talented friend who had the misfortune in his career to consistently win and then lose jobs. He was chewing the drapery one day about it in frustration and cried out, "I work hard—I like to work hard! I deserve better than this." Another friend turned and said, "But you don't work smart. It doesn't matter if you deserve a job—that's no guarantee you'll get it or keep it. Half the people in business don't deserve their jobs; they got them by knowing how to play the game."

This cynical comment has some truth. Many highly talented and deserving people get shuffled out because they have no insight into the mechanics and interactions of business. Many people of, shall we say, less than stunning talents rise up and up through corporate hierarchies because they know the right things to say and do on a political level. There is no such thing as gravitating to the top on merit alone; of being able to maintain a long-term career in a company or companies without a lot of focus and effort and working smart. You have to develop a feel for what people need to hear, learn to do and say the right things with your peers and superiors, and take advantage of situations that most people find intolerable and frustrating and turn them to your advantage.

The friend bewailing his fate above always found it difficult to condone the incompetency of people he worked for and would allow his antagonisms to show through his excellent work. When the chips are down people in power prefer to promote people they feel comfortable with, not someone who is sending out antagonistic vibes. This is their little way of protecting their own turf—they fire the people who make them see their faults, and keep the people who make them look good. If the person being fired happens to be more talented than the one they feel comfy with, well, that's the way the world goes round.

This is not to play down the value of creative talent. Corporations certainly want to hire the best people they can find and give jobs to people with good minds. Very talented people are generally recognized and rewarded, but they still must have a working knowledge of the business of business if they want to maintain their positions in the long run. Since so much of what we call doing business is really politics and diplomacy, no one can afford to rely totally on talent as a survival tool in the corporate world. Too many young people currently entering the job market are not schooled in the matters of human interaction, etiquette and just plain respect for the space of others. The sudden disappearance of social skills has come as a jolt to people as young as thirty-five years old who suddenly are faced with an influx of new employees who don't know the rules. Knowledge of how to interact with different types of people at all levels is essential to corporate success.

When you start out you have to know how to deal with superiors. You must respect the fact that their egos are tied up in their achievements. Later on you need to know how to deal with people under you, and to respect the fact that their egos are tied up in their desire for success and acceptance. And at every level you reach you must deal with your peers and bear in mind that their egos are as important to them as yours is to you. No matter how hot you are at any given moment, and no matter how constant your success remains throughout, you can never afford to overlook the fact that each person you deal with has an ego that must be respected. Management skills are primarily based on that fact.

If you want to learn the nuts and bolts of being a boss, if you need to be shown how to do the jobs you obtain as you are moved up and up, then you must deal with people who can show you. It makes life so much simpler if those people want to help you.

It is also important to be ready to take the reins of management when they are handed to you. Much of this is done by asking questions of people who already hold such positions while you are waiting for your move up. Most people like to give advice—unless the person is so insecure that the idea of giving out information scares the devil out of him. Always ask questions when you're young; and don't be afraid to ask them when you've already had a modicum of success and advancement, as well. This is how you find out how things are done. It's also a good way to make friends, get to know people who can help you, and display your own talents—or stupidities if you don't have any talent. This is how you learn about deadlines, production schedules, paperwork, budgeting, how much money is available for things, who's in charge and who's really running things.

People who exhibit a real interest in the business are also showing how interested they are in their own careers. This is an important aspect of moving ahead—displaying the fact that you *want* to move up. There is a psychological message in this display that even corporations pick up on. They tend to pass over people who don't seem to want to move up. You have to let your goals be known, put some energy behind your fantasy and spark some enthusiasm in your career in someone besides yourself. Always remember that people have a natural desire to want to help people who have a real desire to make it. Very seldom does anyone come beating down an employee's door to get him to take a promotion. It usually goes to the person who is suing for the job himself.

This book covers the patterns currently extant in business today. For the person who wants to take control of his or her rise in the corporate structure, we have put together a framework of situations with advice on how to handle them if you want to find success in your career. Not everyone wants to move to the very top of the heap, but everyone would feel a lot better about being close to that apex. Here we have set forth methods and guidelines on how to get there.

CHAPTER **1**

The Success Focus

Some people want to make fortunes; others want to make fortune cookies.

—LINE FROM A CHINESE FORTUNE COOKIE

THERE IS ONE key to success without which you can't hope to move up very far in the corporate world. The key is focus: you must have a clear goal in mind if you want to get ahead. If you don't know where you want to go it will be impossible to get anywhere. Even if you have a lot of creative talent, you must have the ability to focus and channel your energies if you want the credit, money and prestige that should go with it.

There is nothing new about this idea of focusing and channeling, but it seems there are fewer people entering the business world these days who know how to use it. We live in a fairly indulgent society where so many things have been done for us that our growing-up periods turn out to be studies in how to use all the things available rather than how to create things for ourselves. As a result many people start out not knowing how to cut a career from a job opportunity. The business world is still a part of the natural world where survival of the fittest is the rule. Nothing is given to anyone who does nothing. If you have been raised as a person who has been provided with everything except the need to compete, the business world may seem rather puzzling to you. You can waste years trying to figure out why things aren't being handed to you before you realize that you have to make a play for what you want.

It is not so difficult to get a first job somewhere, but it can be very frustrating to get into a field that you really want. This is often because you are unable to focus on a specific goal, or you may be approaching your goal in the wrong way. For many people the first job determines career choices. If you get into a certain field you may like it enough to pursue it in a real way, and this becomes a new goal. If you get into a field you thought you wanted, but find you hate it after all, you'll be best advised to reassess your previous goals and look for new ones.

Young people just out of school often don't have enough input based on experience to make clear-cut choices. Very often such hard-edged decisions are born out of putting some time in on a job. For example, a person who has majored in a general field of English and psychology may naturally gravitate to publishing and television, or public relations. After spending a year or two at a job in any of these fields the person may decide that he or she is strongly attracted to the challenge and financial rewards of advertising—specifically, selling ad space and bringing in new clients for the company. Then a switch can be made based on real knowledge of the business he or she is in. The person has more ability to make the necessary contacts and decisions that are crucial to such a career shift.

Now, when this person was job hunting for an entry-level position, he or she may have naturally gravitated to a job in the writing or research areas of these firms. His college experience may have led him to feel that such jobs were best suited to his educational background. The first job, however, opened up an area that he may not have been aware of: his desire to express his personality more freely, his wish to interact with a variety of people, his desire to be in an area that was tougher, more aggressive and perhaps had the tang of being more challenging and less secure. Perhaps the bait of being able to increase his income based on his ability to sell was like May wine to him. Such inducements could not be known until some time had been spent learning the business from the inside. The nice thing about focusing on your goals this way is that you have the feeling you've made a "right" move, based on knowledge and insight rather than just a clicking along a prearranged track.

Here the person also makes the decision on self-analysis on the job, not on an academic hypothesis. Experience matures the person, and you can see which of your skills are going to get you what you want in life, and which are going to put you into a boring, dead-end slot. When you see what life really has to offer in the way of career goals you may be horrified at the lack of candyland available, or you may see the truth—that candyland is available to anyone who wants to make it.

Unless you have been to a school that imitates life—such as law school or medical school—you aren't likely to have much of an idea of what is expected of you in an office setting, or even of what the nuts-and-bolts operation of your chosen career will entail. This is why it's good to try to get some practical experience by seeking jobs during summer breaks in companies that offer jobs in what you think your area will be. This will help you decide in college what your focus will be after graduation. Some very intelligent graduates run into career snarls when faced with the corporate situation. Perhaps they have been so focused on being brilliant scholars that they lost sight of the great beyond after graduation. The ones who know the territory have the edge. No matter which type you are, your real goals are verified by your first job and your subsequent decisions to follow up on opportunities that come to you.

Entry Levels

Just about all companies make room for first-timers and are sincere in wanting to help entry-level people become successful.

Some companies are humane in the way they go about this, while others take on new graduates in job lots and keep the best, toss out the rest. There are some individual executives who make a personal policy of interviewing entry-level people as a matter of course, whenever possible. I had one boss who did this, reasoning that he would have a file of potential talent on hand should jobs open up. He also had the admirable intention of helping young people through these interviews to gain confidence and an insight that would help them formulate their career goals.

In any event, a first job provides an opportunity for young people to make contacts, even if the job does not work out in the long term. If the company does not provide much in the way of training or help, it is up to the individual to take the initiative and ask questions, seek help from bosses and colleagues and carve out a personal network of friends and knowledge.

It is important to stress here that if a job is not working out, neither the neophyte nor the boss should try to force the issue. Too many times a young person who is intelligent but weakly motivated will deceive himself and his boss into thinking he should keep on trucking, despite obvious flaws. On the boss's part, it is easier to go with a known quantity of a passable sort than to train someone new. For the employee, those first years out of college are difficult, and he or she may cling to a comfortable situation out of a need for the kind of security that imitates college life. But with this kind of inertia the situation will eventually deteriorate. The employee will become disillusioned and finally drift away in confusion; or a new boss—or the present one—will finally see that the person has failed to achieve an acceptable level of ability, and he will be fired.

Again, let objectivity be the guide, no matter how unpleasant the prospect of looking for a new job may be. It's better to stick to your goals early in your career so you can have an easier time later on.

DO: Maintain a certain flexibility in your demands early on, since many jobs have hidden benefits that you won't see until you've worked there awhile.

DON'T be afraid to rethink your career goals during these early months at the entry level.

Focusing and Channeling

Some people have what might be called a natural focus. They know what they want and just go after it. Others who do not have this clear-minded approach must make decisions based on self-examination, research and sometimes trial-and-error job hunting. Other people may know what they want but have such an emotional intensity about wanting it that they become mired in the wanting instead of moving clearly toward the having. Too much time spent in an emotional quagmire of wishful thinking eats up the energy you should be putting into getting to know people, learning where opportunities lie and building your reputation as a good worker and an energetic person.

Many people think focusing on a goal means screwing up the face and thinking and wishing real hard for something, sort of like the kid who wants a bike for Christmas. In reality focusing means simply knowing what it is you want in your career, then channeling your activities along lines that will logically take you to jobs and companies that will help you realize your goal.

Channeling your energies means learning the skills and mental processes that will help you make the correct choices in your corporate sojourn. Primary among these skills is learning what motivates people, having a clear view of how people react to you, and learning how to select and discard those opportunities that come your way so you don't waste time. You should bear in mind always that it is all right to make mistakes on the way to the top. Mistakes are part of the game. Your overall effectiveness and productivity is the thing you are judged on. You can even make serious, even disastrous mistakes, and not lose your job, as long as you have established yourself as being the kind of employee whose overall worth makes it valid to support you during these times of error.

"Learning people" is the hardest thing for some people to do, although it shouldn't be. First of all, remember that in the office, as in other places, you build support for yourself through your attitude. People like nice people, and want to help and support them. They like to see nasty loudmouths get fired. That is a basic guideline.

Second, remember that people are motivated first by the desire to keep their jobs. Do not make threatening moves in that area. People also want primarily to be accepted by anyone they come into contact with. That's one reason they want to keep their jobs: it means acceptance by their peers. Security and acceptance: these are the two things that every co-worker, boss or employee you come into contact with wants and needs. It's biological as well as psychological. Whatever small or large action you take that soothes or meets those needs will help you get ahead and get along.

Security may be boosted by being asked for advice. Young people who ask for advice from someone already there are subconsciously reinforcing that person's feeling of self-worth on the job, and making him relax. Politeness helps, too. By smiling, saying "Thank you," making pleasantries, you are passing on a subliminal "I like you" to the people you are being nice to. They will then feel accepted and feel a positive warmth for you when they see you. You will be accepted in return. There is no mystery to building support in business for your efforts. You do your work well and be nice to people, and that's at the heart of your success. It's not the *whole* picture, but it's the base coat.

If you have problems cutting into a career, and you are at least fairly sure of what you want, you should always ask for help. Ask for advice from your own boss. Seek out seminars and courses that can refine your judgment and enable you to take advantage of bargaining positions. Read professional journals. Too many people stop studying when they start their first jobs. Make friends in the business so that you know what is current in your profession. This will help you aim your sights more precisely. And always be sure you are going after something that will facilitate your reaching your goals.

DO: Make efforts to prove yourself at entry levels. You have the prerogative of youth to make minor mistakes. If your intentions are good let them show.

DON'T be afraid to rely on tried-and-true methods of etiquette to get people to like you. The reason they are tried and true is that they work.

Early Choices

The basic question a young person must ask is whether or not to compete in the corporate situation at all. After that the decision is whether or not to compete for executive power. After all, not everyone must sit at the top of the corporate heap to be a success. It is important to remember that fact throughout your career. Opportunities will be offered to anyone of proven worth, and each new offer should be seen as another proving ground, not as a final prize. Even if you come to a spot and decide you are not really interested in climbing higher in the corporate structure, you must continue to make choices that will allow you to grow, not stagnate, at that level.

You must never fall into the attitude that you have finally arrived at a spot where you can sit back and cash in your chips. Every position in a company must be occupied by someone who wants to work, not someone who wants to bask. This fact is essential to survival in the business world.

If it seems odd to be discussing such matters as early choices it is because you must learn from the start basic job attitudes that you will utilize and refine throughout your career. If you happen to move ahead quickly when young, you may need to reflect on your career choices sooner than you think. The age of thirty-two is not too early to be making such decisions in business.

DO: Give yourself the chance to move up by saying yes as much as possible to extra assignments, projects, anything that will provide you with more insight and experience on which to firm up your career focus.

DON'T pull back from a career out of insecurity, dislike of a particular job or company or some bad starts. The more you focus on your goals, the better things will get. Some people have to put in time on dreary jobs before finding one at a place they really can like. Once you're there it all seems worth it.

How Large a Company?

Will a large or small company provide the best training ground for your early positions? Large companies can provide not only good learning experiences for the bright young person but more opportunities for movement as you grow. You can move laterally within the same company if you decide to change fields, for example, without leaving the people who know you. Then you can move upward as well because you have remained a proven talent in the company.

Large companies often allow new people to have more time to learn without great pressures; and because there are more people to do the work in general, you don't become swamped by so much work early on that you can't make clear decisions. In a large company a bright person is more visible to influential people, so he can make more powerful friends, as well as have access to information about advancement opportunities. In a small company the young executive may be isolated, or be working too hard to be able to keep well abreast of opportunities at other places. In a small company, indeed, there may be little space for any real career movement.

On the other hand, many large companies like the idea of hiring people who start in small, understaffed companies where they had to perform in a lot of different jobs. Such people have a wider range of experience and talent, and have day-to-day interaction with people ranging from messengers to company heads. Such people may be feistier, more aggressive and more hardworking than those who had a limited amount of variety in their jobs with large companies.

If you want to move ahead quickly, a small company can hold you back simply because you need to be seen. Although there are jealousies in large companies as well as small, there is more room to counter such enemies in a large company. If you run into enemies in a small company you may lose out because there is less space to avoid them, and fewer people to align yourself with against them. In a large company someone who wants to discredit you would have to deal with other equally powerful people who might be well-disposed toward you or who understand the nature of your detractors because there are more people to evaluate both of your personalities. In a small company such an enemy may have credibility simply because there is no one to point out his negative qualities.

This can work against you in another way as well. In a small company you may be the hotshot talent because there is no one else to dim your luster—you stand tall in a mown field. In a large company there is more and better competition to make you continually hone your corporate skills as you move to the top. You end up as a better talent.

It may be that you want to be big in a small company. You may not want to waste time having to compete when you have the opportunity to build a strong position in a small company and turn it into a good thing for yourself. Some people like the freedom of a small company because they want to develop their own managerial styles. Larger companies may require—even dictate—a uniform management style. If you are a street fighter you may do better in a place where informality is better suited to your temperament. In a larger company it is usual to observe the hierarchy and protocols of executive levels; in a small company such formalities may or may not exist, and you may chat as casually with your boss's boss as with your colleagues.

This latter attitude was illustrated to me in one of my early jobs when I was walking by the office of the president-founder-owner of the company. His door was open and I happened to look in; he was somewhat famous because of his career, and I had never met him. He looked up, smiled and said, "Hi, you're new here." I stopped, went in and introduced myself, and we chitchatted awhile about who he was, who I was, ethnic backgrounds and such. After I left I never had the feeling I had overstepped, even though he maintained a benignly aloof status in my mind.

In this same company, which wasn't without influence despite its size, I was able to have regular informal chats with all the top brass and we were all on a first-name basis with one another. When an opportunity arose for a new publication, the editorial director meandered in one day and asked if I wanted it. He never thought it might be more correct to check with my boss first—although she had a few choice words to say to him about it later. If a protocol had had to be observed I might never have heard of the opportunity, or would have had to "arrange" to make it known that I was open to courtship behind her back.

DO: Assess your own needs and demands against those of larger companies and those of smaller companies.

DON'T isolate yourself in any case. Visibility is one of the keys to success.

Pressures to Consider

Are pressures greater in a large company or a small one? In truth they are different pressures. A small company, for instance, may not require a dress code to be observed or that you refrain from telling your boss's boss to knock it off when he starts haranguing. But it may demand ungodly amounts of work and be shy about giving raises. Because larger companies are more structured, the pressures are often political. You must observe a company image, act as befits a junior executive in this company, and be more judicious in your verbal observations of corporate decisions. The formality benefits you when it comes to impartial reviews of your performance and in the manner in which raises are given. You may have to adopt more of a cultivated personality, but you may have to waste less time fighting for things that are promised.

In the final analysis it becomes a matter of how you want to expend your energies at work. If you are geared for political advancement and playing by the rules and making big salaries, then large companies would have the edge. If you value creative freedom, being yourself, and like to fight for every dime, smaller companies usually provide such environments. It goes back to figuring which type of place best will nourish your original goals.

DO: Bear in mind that there is no such thing as a job without pressure, with the possible exception of cloistered nun.

DON'T waste time fighting it out at a company where more fighting it out will be the reward.

The Bureaucrats

There is another type of company, which may be small or large, but which runs on a strictly bureaucratic pattern. In such companies, which may come under stricter government regulation, advancements are determined by paperwork, tests and quotas rather than on merit and input. The money may be there, you may like the work and the people who work there as well, but you also may have the feeling that nothing you do is ever worth anything.

If you are the kind of person who needs a lot of human feedback in your work, you should avoid such impersonal situations where other factors besides how well you do your job are considered for promotion. One example of this was a young man in California who worked for one of the telephone companies. He wanted to gain a supervisory job and was told that if he worked overtime for several months he'd stand the best chance, since his supervisor would recommend him for the job. He worked twelve hours a workday for three months, often going ten-day stretches to make his mark; then the job was given to someone else. The company was short of its quota on women supervisors, it turned out, so he had been passed over. Needless to say, he didn't feel much like exerting efforts toward excellence after that.

It is best to check out the methods a company uses to advance and reward its employees, before starting a job. Nowadays many large companies are gravitating toward more uniform methods of promotion to avoid civil-rights lawsuits, but there are some companies—usually those more susceptible to government regulation—that maintain a certain "facelessness" when it comes to promotions and raises.

Most companies have reputations for fairness, chintziness or generosity, which are easy to check out if you do a little research. Many employment agents are straightforward about communicating negative and positive aspects of the companies they handle as well, since they don't necessarily want their clients coming back with snubnose revolvers later on.

The best way to find out how a company promotes and gives raises is to ask the personnel department interviewer at the first meeting—or whoever is talking to you about the job. Before taking a job with a company of any kind, be sure you have a thorough knowledge of how they handle such matters as rewarding their people for a job well done.

DO: Be sure you have the kind of head that can deal with passing written tests to get promotions. Before joining a bureaucratic company be sure you can deal with the kind of seemingly mechanized mentalities that will govern your raises, promotions and methods.

DON'T think that there is no human interaction in such places. Some of the happiest executives you'll meet are those who are able to adapt to such a clear-cut albeit highly programmed situation.

The First Move to Move

The person who receives an invitation from a company to consider a job is in a more powerful position than someone who is actively seeking to move from one company to another. There would seem to be a psychological advantage in being the pursued. The company becomes the wooing party, so to speak, and they must do the bulk of the convincing if they want you badly enough. It is always nice to receive feelers from employers, and it does a lot for your ego, but does it really make any difference in the long run?

If you decide to accept such a job offer, the fact that you were courted will probably enable you to make a salary gain of at least 10 percent over what you may have been able to command had you sought the job first. This would work to your advantage as far as one-upmanship is concerned; but considering the tax bite and the fact that it's better not to be too highly paid at certain executive levels, this may not result in a real material advantage. It depends on what you consider to be more important: power and prestige, or cash on the barrelhead.

Remember, too, that although it's always nice to have more money to take home, it's also necessary to have the clout to be able to implement your ideas and projects. Your career is to be based on achievements, and when you're moving up it's best to seek out jobs that will enable you to build up an impressive block of accomplishments. When you're bargaining for a new position, this should be one of the things you ask for. It can be more important, in the long run, than a big raise.

It is also important not to become dazzled by the fact that someone is actively trying to get you to make a move to his company. The problem of ego among young executives can become a blinding factor. You may make a wrong move just because you're carried away by the fact that someone is so hot for your corporate body that he will make all sorts of offers to get you to take a job. Here is where you must view your talents objectively, not start believing the flattery you are receiving. In the executive area, as in any other carnival, you must be wary of the hard sell. Check out a company's stability and the reputation (personal) of the executive who is courting you so doggedly, and ask friends for an honest appraisal of your own real talents.

Take this as an example: A bank vice-president was being courted by the president of a small, up-and-coming bank, who acted as though he couldn't live unless this veep came to work for him. He would call twice a day, not unlike a lovesick suitor, dangling promises of perks, pay and power, and generally trying to force the issue to a fast closure.

The bank veep—the courted one—was flattered to distraction and was about to capitulate and render up his corporate charms, when a friend took him firmly by the arm and sat him down to a serious lunch. He pointed out that the veep was about to give up a carefully paced career that had taken him to the right places within the right frames and now he was going to let flattery nuke it all out of existence.

This courting approach was not professional, he pointed out. Research might indicate that the man was erratic, wanted to play big shot, and did not have a realistic viewpoint of what his small bank could offer. Even though the money and position seemed to be a giant advance, in the long run the veep would move ahead better and faster if he waited until he had better experience and moved around in his present corporation. Not only was he in danger of becoming stuck in a no-movement position, and in a place where he would be overpaid and overpositioned and where he could not get broad experience, but the man who wanted him had a reputation for extremely demanding, frustrating behavior.

The lunch was a godsend. The young veep declined. A few months later the president was onto some other project and the veep would have been out of a job himself.

DO: Weigh carefully job offers that might place you at the top too soon, with nowhere to go.

DON'T lose sight of your goals and don't let yourself be taken in by a fast talker. There's also something about all that glitters not being gold, but why indulge in overkill?

Am I My Resumé?

If you are seriously interested in maintaining movement in your career, you should keep your resumé fresh. Whether or not you should keep it strictly honest is between you, your conscience and the fact that nobody is going to spend that much time checking out the fine points anyway. If you're doing your job well or better than average, and you know you can handle whatever curve ball a new job will throw your way, you can relax. There is never any reason to falsify facts, but I've never seen a resumé where a person confessed that his on-the-job effectiveness as a manager was hampered by his abrasive manner, either.

"Dovetailing" job experience so that it gives the impression that you've been steadily employed since graduation is not unacceptable. Deleting jobs of short duration and expanding your time on the jobs before and after is also nothing to chew your nails about. A resumé should be considered something that presents you in the best possible light, without initiating a grassroots movement to have you beatified. It should give a realistic summing up of your experience, but more importantly it should provide a picture of your current capabilities. It should impress the reader enough so that you are a welcome applicant for a job, but should not be so glorifying that your actual presence will be a letdown.

A resumé should never be more than two pages long, and many people feel that one and a half pages is more than adequate. If you have great experience, concentrate on the most recent or current position and hammer that home; then just give dates, places and positions on the previous jobs unless you have some special accomplishment that should be brought up. No one cares overly much what you did in college unless you founded SDS—in which case they probably know as much about it as you do. People are also not likely to be fascinated by the fact that you knocked around Europe bumming pfennigs for a year after college; nor should you mention that you studied at Actors Studio if your present position in life is control manager at a data-processing firm.

Besides making you look good, a resumé should tell an interviewer what he or she wants to hear. Don't send your resumé to places for jobs you are clearly overqualified for. Make sure your resumé tells people that you can do what they are looking for someone to do. It is not recommended that you waste resumés by taking long shots on jobs you really don't want but are applying for because you need the money. People can read through such actions by the quality of your experience, and since few people in the business world are doing charity work they aren't about to give you a job just because you need one. It is much better to sling hash awhile for some extra cash than to make a career move downward during a lean time. There is in fact nothing shameful about an out-of-work exec taking a job as a bartender to keep from losing his mortgage between career moves. Lillian Hellman worked as a clerk in a department store when the IRS was being ugly to her during the McCarthy years, and this was well after her major successes. I always feel if she could do it, so can anyone else. If you won't do things to survive because of pride, then you probably won't do that well in the business world anyway.

Back to resumés and what they hold.

If you did work in a deli or a bar during a bad time, there is no reason to put it on your resumé. You can always say you took a sabbatical, or you free-lanced during that time, or did consulting work.

Companies may want to know the following on a resumé:

- What do you do?
- Where did you learn to do it?
- For whom have you done it and for how long?
- Marital status. This may be positive information if the corporate spot involves a lot of socializing; or negative if the job involves a lot of travel or overly long hours. If you feel it's negative avoid mentioning it.

Impressive military background is a plus if the company deals with government contracts; otherwise there isn't much reason to go into detail about it on a resumé. If you started out aiming at a military career and changed your mind to go into the private sector, of course it becomes part of your overall experience.

Reasons for leaving a job are usually not listed, since it is normally assumed you left one place to go to another. It may come up in the interview, however, and when it does you should not present personal disagreements as a reason for leaving, and you should never knock a former employer. If you left under adverse conditions, you can say that it was time to move on. Unless the interviewer asks directly if he can contact the former employer, you should not offer any negative comments about why you left. When pressed to the wall, however, you can say that your personal relationship with the former employer is not such that you would care to have him contacted, and provide the name of someone who you feel would give a better picture of your qualifications. You don't have to admit you were fired unless your former boss might tell. You should have a pretty valid reason for wanting to leave a job that you still hold. First, you probably won't be able to let the interviewer contact the present boss, and, second, people want to know whom they are hiring and what problems may be repeated on the new job. You may have very positive reasons for wanting to leave, and they should be stated. But even negative reasons, such as lack of money or disenchantment with the company, should be expressed in noncomplaining terms and viewed as a good boost for getting you out of a possible rut.

If you are being fired, be as candid as is prudent. If you ripped off several thousand dollars of computer equipment, sold corporate secrets or aided a band of teenage computer whiz kids, you can bank your software that it will show up in a printout somewhere along the line.

DO: Keep your resumé fresh. Reread it every eight months or so and see how it sounds. If it holds up, keep it; if it embarrasses you, read it again a week later, and if it still needs work, rework it.

DON'T give a potential interviewer outlandish lies for consideration. Everybody goes through the same trial by fire during the years of entry into business. Provide a framework for the interviewer to help you arrive at a decision about whether or not you want to work at the job.

Getting Interviewed

One of life's less pleasant situations is the job interview—for both the job seeker and the interviewer. Part of the bugaboo is that no one ever really knows what to talk about during these sessions. At the very heart of the matter a job interview boils down to two people trying to decide if they like each other enough to work together. To arrive at this simple evaluation the two must spend an awkward half hour together asking questions that may or may not have answers, at least not until some time has been spent working together.

Whether you are on a first-time job hunt or come bearing experience, the pattern remains the same, and, mostly, so do the questions. The interviewee should have ready answers to these kinds of questions:

- What kind of background—educational or professional—do you have that makes you a contender for the job at hand?
- Are you really interested in pursuing this line of work in a serious way, or are you just looking for something to pay the rent until Michael Jackson asks you to marry him?
- How much money do you want to do this job?
- How much money will you settle for instead?
- What are your career goals?

When going after any job, but especially your first job, you will have a better interview—if not a better chance at getting the job —if you rehearse possible answers to such questions the night before. Many people take the time to make sure that their clothes are clean and pressed, that the shoes match the clothes and the hair is on straight, but few sit down for a half hour and calmly make a list of assets and career purposes so that they can offer information to the interviewer. It is difficult to imagine you impressing an employer with your success focus if you sit in tense silence and offer minimal, mealymouthed responses to questions that give you an opportunity to sell yourself.

The Big Question

To return to that crucial question about what you want to do with your life, the answer, put in general terms, is this: "I want to move into such-and-such a field and I feel—or hope—that this job will give me the background I need to advance in that area. I also feel that this company [if it does] has enough opportunities to help me move toward that goal."

Now, if the interviewer turns out to be a tricky s.o.b. and says, "How do you know that about this company?" you will have to provide some knowledge about the place—its size, its product, its standing in its field. You can get some of this information from an employment agency, or from company brochures, or at the library, or from business magazines. There is nothing wrong with stopping by and asking the personnel department for company literature some days before the interview, or stopping by early for your appointment and asking the receptionist if there is any company literature you might peruse in preparation for the interview.

Remember this: You are there to do what you can to get the job offer. You are not making a legal commitment to a career just because you told an interviewer you have a certain goal in mind. Your immediate goal is to get the job. Your next step is to decide whether or not to take it. And your next step after that is to utilize the job to facilitate your own personal career goals.

DO: Rehearse the night before so you will have a basis of things to talk about. This will help you be yourself.

DON'T be afraid to be enthusiastic. Interviewers need your energy on which to base their questions. Give the interviewer something "up" to link to, to enjoy.

First-Timers

If nothing else, the entry-level job seeker should be able to elaborate briefly on the question: Where do you want to go in your career? Now, most young people find this question the poser of all time, since few of them actually *know* the answer to that question. Invent an answer. You must know something about your college background, it being so very fresh in your mind. Why did you study English lit? To help you communicate with words? Or psychology? Because it would help you understand human behavior and motivation so that you would eventually be a better management executive?

The first-timer must understand how his educational background can be applied to the corporate picture. Remember that your first job will provide you with a working knowledge of your company's area of commerce. You don't have to come to a job interview with a working knowledge of the business. It should not be too difficult to prime yourself on the company's products and who uses them before going on an interview. If you have a technical background, you will of course have an easier time presenting yourself for a job at a company that makes computers. If you have a liberal-arts background, with some business courses and some experience working on school publications, you may have a harder time trying to figure how to mesh that background with a future television career.

The thing to remember is that most places of business utilize similar basic production methods, and that whatever you did in college will relate somehow to business. The point of the job interview is to ask questions and give answers that will bring this out. The people who are most impressive at job interviews are the kids who are secure in their backgrounds and goal orientation and aren't afraid to state it positively. Always bear in mind that a college grad is not expected to have a lot of experience; only that he has the ability to maximize the background and part-time experience he does have to offer.

Your Questions

Whether fresh from college or previously employed, anyone being interviewed for a job can provide a positive image of himself if he asks as many questions as he answers. Remember that some executives don't have any trained ability for gathering information from a job seeker so the job seeker has to provide it. If you are the kind of person who can initiate much of the chitchat when the interviewer peters out, you will earn some points for taking the onus off him.

Some areas you may ask about:

- Duties of the job. Ask what exactly you will be expected to do on a day-to-day basis.
- Side duties. Will there be some surprises for you about taking up slack from other employees, answering phones, filling out forms?
- Advancement opportunities. Will this job take you upward in the company, or will you do this job for years waiting for someone to die off so you can move up?
- Salary. Ask about money candidly. How much does the job pay, and what is the pattern of salary increments? You should go to the interview with a clear picture of how much you need to live on; if the job is not going to support you, you may not be able to consider it. Some people feel that the discussion of money should wait until some interest is expressed by the employer, then negotiate for a feasible amount. This is true, perhaps, at higher levels, where one has a better knowledge of what to expect and is more likely to bargain for other things first, but the neophyte should know what the going rate is for a job as soon as possible. Besides, it's good practice to view one's financial worth candidly early in the game.

DO: Be direct. If you want the job, focus on that. Don't fudge on it, don't be shy about wanting it. Provide a no-mistake attitude that you belong with the company and you should have the job. Point out every little thing that's relevant to the fact that you should be The One.

DON'T forget that the interviewer will like it a lot if you are The One so that he can quit talking to The Others sooner.

Postinterview Thoughts

It is important, though not always financially feasible, *not* to take a job out of desperation at the start. You will have to expend a lot of time and energy learning the job and doing your work. If it is not a job that will take you into an area you want or that you enjoy, it may drain energy from you that could be better used to continue looking for a job you would really like. You may end up feeling that the background in a nonrelated job will work against your getting into your preferred field.

Remember that first jobs are at least job experience, even if in a nonrelated field. Also, all office situations imitate one another to some extent, so the fact you are employed at all will work in your favor. If you must take a job you don't want, it is imperative to keep looking for one you prefer. Continue sending out resumés to promising places. Since you have an income, you can be more selective now anyway. Get together or keep together with a good employment agency and emphasize what types of jobs you want, and interview only for those ones. Send letters of inquiry with your resumé to companies you would like to join.

If you luck out and the job does have merit for you, review these questions:

- How long will you be able to stay at this company and gain from it?
- How much advancement probability is there? Here the age level of the other staff people is a

consideration, and that can be brought up in the interview. If it's a young staff holding heavy-duty jobs, they're likely to keep them for a while. If they're older, a younger person will be able to gain more of a foothold sooner.

- Is the company expanding or stagnant? A dynamic firm in a healthy industry will most likely open up new jobs for smart young people who want to move up faster. Old established places may expect a time-stop movement and take a more conservative approach to your youthfulness.
- What does the money look like? If it's disappointing, rest assured it won't get better. Money never does in places that like to keep compensation limited. Never minimize the importance of that fact. The struggle to get money can eat up a lot of creative energy.

DO: Discuss fringe benefits at the first job interview if it seems that you are being received in a positive way and if you are seriously interested in the job. If you aren't, don't waste time in idle chitchat.

DON'T waste time going on job interviews at companies you clearly would not want to work for. Also avoid areas that make your stomach wrench when you hear about them.

Taking the Job

To continue a theme, do not be shy about asking for adequate money for a job at any level. Don't fudge on it, or let it slide, or allow yourself to be talked into less than you have been led to believe was available. If they are offering a certain salary for a job, then they can afford to pay it to you, period. If you're not worth the full amount, then why are they hiring you at all? Don't accept the idea that you are somehow second class. If, for example, you have been told a job pays $15,000 a year, and you get an offer of $13,000, then ask what happened to the original amount.

Never go into any job feeling uncomfortable about the money you settled for. There are few resentments that can spoil a job more effectively than feeling you were somehow ripped off. Financial compensation is a big part of a satisfying career and should be incorporated reasonably into your success focus.

At any level it is important to get your money, perks and contracts up front. Never bank on raises that will be "coming down the road," in six months or after a review of how you're working out. If a company can't afford your services when they're trying to impress you they certainly won't go to any effort to reimburse you once you've been working for them for six months.

Other factors to think of when considering a job are prestige, opportunity and creative satisfaction. Many companies who have great names offer that in lieu of financial compensation. They figure that having worked there you will be more valuable on the market when you look for other jobs. The problem here is that it's difficult to move to a less prestigious company after having the taste of fame. Still, it is a valid consideration, depending on the field you're in. Just remember that your landlord and the telephone company have only marginal interest in the fame of your company's name. They prefer the reputation of the U.S. dollar.

Creative satisfaction and opportunity: now, these are very solid compensatory areas, since you can learn a lot and can eventually make up the financial amount at a time when it really will matter. When taking any job, consider these areas as studiously as you do any other consideration.

DO: Try to take a job that provides an atmosphere you would want to spend eight or more hours a day in.

DON'T forget that just because you can't eat glamor for breakfast it doesn't follow that it has no value at all. If all other things—or a nice portion of them—are there, glamor can help swallow the rest sometimes. At least temporarily.

Running Not Scared

One killer of success motivation is fear of losing one's job. Everybody is afraid of losing his job—even people who are not fearful on a conscious level. It's a basic survival trait; it's biological, perhaps. It is normal to want to hold on to something good—even something bad if it pays well. If you want to maintain control of your success focus, you must conquer this fear of losing what you have.

To maintain your success focus, you must retain self-confidence, and this comes primarily from an objective view of your own talents and abilities. If you rely on emotions and ego, you can fall into the trap of holding on to a job because it's there. You identify with it instead of with yourself. You forget that the job is as much what you make it as what it allows you to do. A basic danger to anyone's motivation is identifying too strongly with any one position or company. You must always identify yourself as an entity who is allied with a company doing a certain job—brilliantly, of course.

If you hang on to a job—fall in love with it, so to speak—you can halt your own growth, and perhaps lose your ability to continue moving in the direction you have set for yourself. Goal changing is one thing; goal killing is something you do not want to get into.

Such holding on seems to afflict enormously successful people at what might be called middle-level positions. They have enough clout to do what they want creatively and make good salaries and reputations for themselves. Suddenly the glamor of it all hits them and they don't want to let go of the job that "made them," even if they move up. Their security, their identity, has become tangled up in that job and they start losing the confidence that they can keep it.

The thing to remember from your early days onward is that

there is no such thing as a famous job—except, maybe, for Queen of England. It has been shown over and over that a talented person makes the job highly desirable, not the other way around. Any job should be viewed as an opportunity for a talented person to sparkle.

> **DO:** Maintain a sense of yourself at all times.
>
> **DON'T** forget there is a world outside your bailiwick. If your job is supergood, maybe you made it that way.

Horatio Alger–Like

Even today it is still true that you can start out as mailroom attendant or secretary—or anywhere in what may be called the bedrock of a company—and move up to a high-power position. I have several examples of this sort of thing ready at hand to show on request. My favorite is the man who went from chorus dancer in the movies to mailroom boy to salesman of precious metals to second in command of his firm in eight years. He was still under forty, had no formal education along corporate lines, and ended up with an expense account and a company-paid car.

We mention this here only to give encouragement to the depressed and the disillusioned. It doesn't matter if you think you are in a rut in your career; if you want to change and move up quickly, look for opportunity, ask for help, don't worry about what your resumé says—just go after it. You can have the best credentials in the world; if you don't have the guts and the goal—and most of all the true desire for success—you can forget it. You must never talk yourself out of advancement by prejudging yourself before you try. If you want something, get someone to spruce your resumé into a streamlined thing, and send it to every place, answer every ad, in the area you want until you start getting responses. The old Dale Carnegie approach still works: think positively about yourself and you'll convince someone to give you a chance. But you have to have the guts to go after it in the face of adverse conditions.

Creativity and Clout

Decisions often become blurred when highly creative people are offered rewards—which are usually defined corporately as being moved into an administrative position. Here some strong choices must be made. It is almost impossible to refuse an offer of advancement when building a career; indeed, few people even question whether or not to take such an offer. The decisions here are not so much whether to accept an offer that will place you in an administrative job, as how to arrange things to maintain your creative versatility while gaining corporate power as an executive.

Many creative people who get into the big-money-and-power positions feel tremendous disappointment. Now they are watching other people have the fun creating while they say yes or no to their employees. This is the time to redefine what one calls "creativity." The truly versatile person of this stripe finds that he or she can rechannel creative patterns into influencing, setting styles and helping younger creative people develop along new lines.

The point here is never to allow your goals to become set in concrete. Always find new channels for your creative flow and allow your goals to mature with your upward progress.

It should be fulfilling creatively to have newer creative people adopting your patterns and viewpoint into their work as it is to come up with new ideas yourself. People who set standards and become imitated in business—even at quiet levels—are the ones who survive and who retain clout.

CHAPTER **2**

Taking Aim and Moving In

"... But he doesn't know the territory!"

—LINE FROM MEREDITH WILLSON'S *The Music Man*

AN ECONOMICS PROFESSOR who had a real passion for money told me once that you should not get to like your job too much, since it could stand in the way of your getting your money. Settling into a job as if it were a permanent home, he felt, kept you from advancing careerwise. Even though this is a narrow view, in many ways he was right. First of all, a job is not a home; it should be a tool by which you advance along the creative lines you've mapped out for yourself. Even if you do stay with one company, the job should still be used in a dynamic way, not as a comfortable old shoe you can't bear to part with.

For most people intent on executive advancement, scouting

the fields of job opportunities is part of the game plan. Again, even if you stay where you are, you must stay aware of the outside world so that you don't lose ground either in promotions or in salary advancement. Some people move around a lot and make a bundle doing it; others cannot afford to risk too much company-hopping on their resumés. It takes a particular personality to get away with a lot of jumping around, and it is acceptable only in certain quirky, volatile areas. If you need to make selective switches to climb up the ladder, you should do so with the proper approaches.

In this chapter you will learn how to maintain your career goals and educate yourself in ways of the business world in which you plan to move.

Now You See Me

If you want to move up in business the first rule is not to be invisible. The problem is how to attain visibility in a way that benefits you. It is easy to be a loudmouth, a jerk, a negative force, and be noticed in that way, but how can you make sure your talents are being seen in a positive light?

First you must make a strong positive impression on your boss, and that is done by performing the job effectively. That means taking each assignment and putting your mind to it so that you do it right. It may involve asking questions of your boss on procedures and results expected, and if it does, don't hesitate to ask. Asking is part of the job. Early in the job you must show your boss you are a worker. That is the key to impressing the boss in the first weeks: performance, and results. Early in anyone's career, the rule should be less talk, more action.

- Educate yourself. Read all correspondence, all interoffice memos. Familiarize yourself thoroughly with your office files, with what's on your boss's desk. Impress him with your knowledge and efficiency.

- Use your initiative. Look at the situation and offer to do things that may need to be done, such as reorganizing files, setting up systems to clear backlog work, ways of handling too many phone calls. Your initiative usually is best received when it effects an improvement in the office area. Find something that needs to be done and offer a way to do it, or do it yourself, if your position warrants it. Remember: anything you create in an office situation makes you that much more valuable, and that much less dispensable.

One young woman heard that a higher-level executive was about to take a trip to her hometown. She quickly made a phone call to him and offered tips on where to stay, where to go and some good restaurants. Since the exec had never visited the town, her advice helped him save time and gave him a good trip instead of a frustrating one.

Not in all companies could the young woman have been able to make herself so visible to an influential higher-up without courting suspicion. It all came from her keeping alert to what was going on in the office *in toto* and having the smarts to comprehend and act on an opportunity. She had developed good working relations with people that others may have avoided, so she knew who was doing what and when. She knew the company was informal enough to allow interaction with high-level executives. She was interested in the company, in her own advancement, and in ways that would let her instruct others in her interests. This is what moving up is all about.

Not all bosses are nice, or benevolent, nor do all bosses like the idea that someone they've hired has a lot of potential to move ahead quickly. Some people, you understand, get a little edgy when they feel threatened. We'll discuss that in a later chapter, but for the moment let's talk about being visible at early stages when you're not quite sure your boss is running the ball for you. You may have a good boss who is as delighted as your parents are about your bright prospects, and who goes forth to make your talents known by giving you credit and mentioning you to higher-ups. Or you may have a boss who recognizes your talents but wants to keep you his own little secret so that he can look like the talent during promotion and raise time, while you are kept underground until February 2. In such a case you must take initiative again and make sure that common knowledge has it that you are the hot new property in your department.

To be noticed by bosses:

DO: Ask questions and offer constructive advice.

DON'T substitute talk for action. Don't be afraid to present your best abilities when the opportunity arrives. Don't be shy.

Making Friends: Guarantees for Visibility

One way to make sure you get due credit is to make friends—friends with your co-workers first. When you get together at lunch or drinks you can mention what you are doing there in the office. It need not be done in such a way that you start in talking about how darn great you are, but when the conversation normally turns to what's happening with work—which it definitely will, since what else are co-workers going to talk about?—you can lightly mention what *you* are doing.

You most certainly should make it a point to have lunch with the people you work with—one needs support in business and you can use the time for a little subliminal advertising. Such as: "I had this idea I gave to John the other day, and he loved it, but I think there's a little missing. What do you think about this? . . " Soon everyone knows which ideas are yours and which are John's, so he will have a harder time taking your credit from you. Don't underestimate the value of common knowledge and the gossip that stems from it.

DO: Talk about what you're doing.

DON'T brag.

Memos Are Demos

Another way to keep your head above water and above ground is to utilize memos, even when you present your ideas orally. Follow up a meeting with a memo summarizing your presentation, and keep a copy for your own files. Make sure all memos are dated. By doing this you will subtly underline to your boss that you have been feeding in ideas and make it more difficult for him to shut you out. It has a strong psychological effect; the power of the printed word acts strongly on anyone's mind. The fact that something is written makes it more yours than your boss's. He will feel impelled to give you some credit somewhere along the line or live with the dread feeling that some ghost in chains will visit his room on Christmas Eve.

It will also make your boss less credible when he tries to take credit for your ideas, and he will not be able to do so quite so smoothly. He may still exhibit his funny ways, but it will put real pressure on him to give you your due.

Another memo ploy is to provide written summarizations of your presentation to your co-workers so that they can hold them while you speak at meetings. This will give them something strong to focus on, and it will be forever implanted in their memories whose ideas are being presented. People also like the idea that this work has been done for them. It comes off as a nice consideration of their sensibilities.

It can also help offset this situation: A young exec had come up with an idea that he presented in a group departmental meeting. The idea was good and was adopted readily. At a subsequent meeting the head of the department presented it as *his* idea to a high-level executive. Since the department was under fire from management, the true byline for the idea would have meant a big boost for the original presenter. Since nothing was in writing, the most the creator of the program could do was widen his eyes in shock at the duplicity of his boss. Later his colleagues whispered that they remembered whose idea it was, but, at that point, so what?

DO: Write everything down and keep copies where no one can get at them.

DON'T rattle off ideas in brainstorming sessions without follow-up memos to the people who were at the meeting.

Learning the Lay of the Land

The interoffice layout may cause some confusion to the person who has never worked in an office before. Even college grads may feel some puzzlement about who does what and who should be cultivated. Again, the best way to learn anything is to ask questions. If a name crops up several times in the first week, you will want to ask someone what the person does and at what level of importance he or she functions.

It is recommended that you read anything interoffice at the beginning until you can select and edit based on experience. This is a way to gain a picture of who and what are happening at your company. It gives you names and titles and things to ask about. It helps you to learn the officers of the company and their names and functions. Many powerful executives have no specific functions, it seems, until the time when you meet them at the Christmas party and don't know how they affect your career.

DO: Ask questions, read memos, earnings reports, newsletters and promotion notices. Congratulate people who have received promotions or commendations. Become familiar with the files, the secretaries, and the people in other departments who have even a passing communication with your own area.

DON'T turn off everything except the specific work you do at your desk. Don't be a nerd. Don't be overly reticent. Don't become insular.

Advertising Yourself

There are two ways to make yourself a household word in your company, and both should be utilized. One is, as we said, to do the work and do it well. The second is to get to know people who should know you. In some companies there is a lot of exchange between people in higher and lower positions, and this is a wonderful way to make friends with people who would be aloof from you in more structured corporations. You can't beat this kind of social interchange for getting yourself known and liked with the biggies. Since they talk to you regularly, they see your faults and assets all at once and are more disposed to accommodate your progress. You are right *there,* so to speak, with the goods and holding out the treat bag when credit is being distributed. When you share a washroom with the president's son, you have a greater opportunity to make a splashier impression.

In more formalized situations you must depend strongly on producing revenues or salable work for the company and gaining access to high-level people in that way. In these kinds of companies there is a "class line" between upper and lower executives, and here is where memos are a way of life—as are reports.

Remember, here's where your name, in writing, counts. In less structured companies where things are generally presented in a family-dinner atmosphere, it is easier to lose track of specifics, and you can even be seen as pushy if you try to take credit for past ideas. In more structured offices, rigid guidelines keep track of the track records; in less formal ones you are dependent on a big amorphous "one happy family" atmosphere to benefit you.

We knew of one company where the boss's son was titular head of a department. One young executive who didn't really want to work much defined his own job as going to lunch and coffee breaks with the boss's son. Every day he would make reservations for them, and if there were any others who had to have lunch with the boss's son this exec arranged it and tagged along. He made a lot of money for a while, but when the boss died and the company was sold, the boss's son was bought out.

There weren't many openings in other companies for this particular position, and the lunch circuit lost a favorite son.

> **DO:** Build a solid basis of accomplishment on which to write your resumé.
>
> **DON'T** ever get the idea that people don't see everything you're doing once you've made yourself visible.

Shop Talk

I once knew of a crazy lady who started rumors about herself so that people would talk about her in business and she could stay visible in that way. Because she was crazy she got away with it. The exchange of information in business is important. It helps to read publications pertaining to the business you are in and to join some professional organizations which meet regularly so that you have a better chance of meeting people who can provide information. Many people resist joining such organizations, but it can't hurt to meet others in your chosen field on a friendly basis to learn what's happening in your business, and to find out about more career opportunities. People prefer to hire and recommend people they are friends with. If no one knows you, how can they recommend you?

Social interactions give you a chance to talk to people who otherwise may be aloof from you during the workday. At a professional luncheon or smoker the bars are removed, however, and some enterprising young executive can meet higher-ups in his own office or an outside company. Also, these places are gossip exchanges—good and bad gossip. For example, if you are being maligned by a bad boss, here is a chance to talk about it to friends, who will talk about it to others. These interactions can expand your horizons and possibly provide you with avenues of escape.

Contributing articles to industry newsletters is a good way to keep your name visible, even if nothing concrete comes of it. It is good to be known as a name in your field, and getting the name printed with items about your activities is one way to do it. Again the printed word lends clout to your name.

> **DO:** Meet people in your field. Arrange social outings, join professional organizations. Let people know you!
>
> **DON'T** isolate yourself and live in a vacuum.

Memos to Yourself

Every workday is a busy one, and you may even be the kind of person who can remember all the things you plan to do in the order in which you plan to do them. Admirable as that quality is, and a useful one in keeping one up on everyone else, it doesn't leave much room for the unexpected. And, as we all know, the unexpected *crise d'office* is what usually happens to keep you from getting to your planned schedule of work. The usefulness of the memo to oneself is that it lets you get back to what you were doing without the frustration of sitting in disarray around 3 P.M. after a hectic day of interruptions wondering what in the devil you were doing when the first shot was fired. No problem: you refer to your list of chores and pick up where you left off.

If you have never used this tool, you may be wondering what we are talking about. The memo to oneself is a sheet of paper that lists all the things you plan to complete or start or check out that day: your assignments to yourself. You keep it handy on your desk or nearby for easy reference. As you complete each task you cross it off and go on to the next thing. Basically it's an organizer, and even the highest-level execs utilize it.

A sample may go like this:

- Set meeting with J. Rosen at Columbus Mfg.
- Get tix for trip to Atlanta.
- Call Sandra for tryst.
- Fire Bob.
- Get present for S.

- Send records to Acct.
- Set up meeting with staff about drop in productivity.
- Have someone order donuts and coffee for said meet.

You may want to arrange the list according to what needs to be done first. Some people prefer separate headings for phone calls, outside appointments, letters, meetings, etc. If you purchase the right sort of day-by-day calendar, the task can be noted directly on it and you'll have one less piece of paper to clutter your desk.

Simple as these memos may seem, they help tremendously to get things done during the day. If your boss keeps these kinds of memos it's a good idea to counter and cover yourself by keeping them yourself. I had a boss who kept little four-by-five-inch memos in a file folder and loved pulling them out at the most inconvenient times to ask why something hadn't been done by such and such a time as you had said on such and such a date. You cannot imagine what a horse's neck truly feels like until you've been caught by one of those memo reminders. They're like getting raspberry seeds caught between your teeth. It's in writing. The only defense against them is to keep countermemos, dated, yourself.

DO: Write a list for yourself as reminders.

DON'T lose it!

Becoming a Resource

As you move along, inquiring, always inquiring, into new ways to make yourself more and more indispensable to your company —and the world around it—you should think of ways to carve out something that is uniquely your own. Not everyone wants to start some new department, of course; many people prefer to shine in established and existing settings. There are those, however, who find something lacking in their jobs and who think of ways to strengthen it.

If you are one of these people, first examine your company's needs. Find an area that is either undeveloped or losing ground, and develop a program to fill the need. Define the new area yourself—around your own talents and hopes for the future, of course—and present it as a new department with you as the head, or as a new position for yourself.

Sometimes this new creation need not be based on an already existing area, but on a whole new concept that you've had in mind for a while. Many people are shy about coming up with a total program, or about presenting such ideas for untried directions, usually because of fear of rejection. This is not a valid reason to avoid presenting an idea. Always assume that if you have something you think is a hot idea, there is someone out there who will feel the same way.

In many cases this is how new companies get started. When some smart exec gets a good idea that his company can't go along with, he or she implements it in a new business, independently. If the company does agree to back up the idea as a new department they will usually back it up fully so that it will have a real chance of success. Naturally it seems that large, rich companies are the best ones to float such new ideas, since their budgets are larger and more flexible, but smaller companies are often also amenable. If you have such an idea, you should present it complete with financial projections and analyses and give it a shot.

In order to establish yourself as a credible idea person in your company you must build a reputation for accomplishment. It helps if you have a higher-level executive in your corner backing you up. You are in essence selling yourself as well as the idea, and you must be a known quantity since your idea is all on paper.

Several examples of the feasibility of such programs are extant. One was in a major cosmetics company. An executive wanted his own division, and there was none available. So he presented an idea for a new line of fragrances and cosmetics based on a famous name in the Italian peerage. He contacted the duchess, got her enthusiastic agreement, presented the idea with plans to market the products to an upscale, high-income woman, and the company bought it. The duchess chose the final fragrance, and it was a go. Although it never made fantastic profits, the line became well established and remains so today.

Another involved two research men who had spent years working on what they considered a dead-end project for a major electronics corporation. Dissatisfied, the two men discovered they could go in a new direction using much of the same research they had been doing. They presented a proposal for a new division to relocate out of their area, and got the go-ahead for a ten-year project, and considerably more money for themsleves. Since they directed the company away from a no-solution project, while utilizing their present research, they were able to head off expensive waste. They rechanneled their energies to focus on something that would have more potential for success.

DO: Look for areas where your company could benefit from growth and development. Think of ways and project those areas that will advance along with your career.

DON'T procrastinate because you aren't sure whether you can do it. They'll tell you if you can't do it. Even if it doesn't work out in the long run, you still will retain your clout because you came up with something everyone thought would work. In this case, lack of success is not necessarily to your detriment.

Creative Flowering versus the Status Quo

Have you ever noticed that everybody wants originality until they're confronted with it? Then they get very nervous and start foofing and humphing about how this or that can't work because it's too radical and no one will buy it. Then about three months later your idea crops up independently in a new product from the West Coast, and *Time* and *Newsweek* start cloning the verbs about how it's going to change the face of your industry. Then those people who foofed and humphed start calling meetings about why there's not this kind of thinking coming out of Foof & Humph Industries.

Sort of makes you want to rethink your adolescent inclination toward a religious vocation.

If you are in a spot where you are not—or feel you are not—being used to your best abilities, you must reevaluate your position, your company and your reasonable expectations to do something valid with your career. There are companies that do stand in the way of ambition, that thwart serious people who want to contribute something valuable to the world via a corporation. I was asked for advice on this very subject by a man who was being held down in a health-care company he worked for in the Southwest.

He worked in a company that had mostly women in the middle power slots, and he had been unable to make any headway. "They constantly ask my ideas and implement them," he said, "then I'm promised promotions and raises, and they don't come through. No one seems to remember the promises when the chips are down and others get promoted."

He wasn't interested in a hearing, but of course this was exactly the kind of thing he needed—a grievance hearing. Nobody should take this kind of holding down. Such a case represents a rip-off of talent by bosses and ultimately by a company. I suggested that the man try writing down all of his ideas and all of the times he'd been promised raises or promotions and date them. Write them down, I told him, then sit down to a meeting with your two supervisors and present the bare facts to them, then ask to have a date set by which the situation would be rectified. If it was not, I suggested he change jobs, or seek a transfer to another department.

The time comes when you must be candid with yourself. Even a job that has a lot of clout and glamor may be keeping you in a stagnant position. You must ask yourself some serious questions if you find yourself not moving and not gaining increases in respect, compensation and job level.

- Why am I not moving? Is it because there is no movement possible in this company, or am I not good enough for the jobs available?
- Am I being kept down because I'm a woman, or a man in a woman-dominated industry, or because my bosses just don't much care one way or the other?
- Have I become too comfortable in the job so that I'm letting opportunities slip away? Am I in fact sacrificing a future because I'm comfortable here, despite the lack of compensation?
- Are my bosses insecure? Are they using my talent for their own gain? Are they competent enough to judge me after all?

Answers to these questions may lead to some shocking and even scary realizations. You may have to rethink your career approach. If you have been going at it like a nebbish, just letting things come or not come to you, then you need to punch up your focus and change your thinking. Get some outside advice from pros. Seek jobs. Answer ads and independently have interviews with other companies. Ask for them. If you want to stay in your own company, start making some positive noises to your bosses and your own personnel people. Ask for advice. Ask for reasons. Present your accomplishments in writing and ask for reasons why you are being passed over.

If you receive negative answers, such as that you aren't really as good as you think, then you must counter with a very obvious response: If you aren't doing the job, why are they keeping you there, why are you working overtime, and why are your ideas being utilized? Any boss who is keeping an incompetent on the job for years is exhibiting incompetence himself.

Usually the problem is not in your talent but in your lack of style. You perhaps do not believe you have much to offer, so you offer your accomplishments as if you don't deserve credit for them. Someone else then automatically takes them from you. There are unscrupulous people who do this, but usually it's done because of some nonaction on your part.

There is that famous phrase in business: Nice guys finish last.

What this means is that easygoing, nonaggressive people don't demand recompense for their work and don't get it. Ask yourself how often you have let the company go without paying its dues to you. How often have you let reviews for raises go unnoticed? How often have you stood quietly while someone else got credit for your work? Like the man above, if you have grievances, why are you afraid to express them?

Develop a positive aggressiveness—it is not a nasty quality, it is the most important business tool you can have.

- Sign all your work.
- Write down all your assignments from the boss and keep them on file. Keep dates on completion.
- Keep tabs on feedback. Is your work being passed on quietly? If work does not come back with complaints, then you must assume the work is good. If it gets no praise, then ask about it.
- If your work is below par, you have a right to know where to make improvements. If it is good or excellent, you should hear about it. If you put a cherry bomb in the men's room, you'd hear about it, all right. Why shouldn't you hear if you're making a big splash of another kind that's making waves on the stockholders' reports?

DO: Keep tabs on how you're doing. Ask.

DON'T whine about things if you aren't getting what you deserve.

DO: Present professional memos about why you deserve promotions and raises and what all.

DON'T hang around too long if the company is too blockish to accommodate your needs.

Early Changes

To continue a theme, you should keep tabs on your company from the first months of your new job. Even first-timers must read the signs if they don't want to get bogged down in the wrong company, even if it's the right career area.

Attitudes are extremely important. Your boss's attitude is the most important. If the boss starts right out the first week expressing dissatisfaction with you, then you must realize that the bozo didn't know what he wanted when he hired you. He never will know what he wants unless you (a) define your job yourself and force it on him; (b) sit him down early on and make him define what he wants so that you can provide it. Usually such bosses are insecure and unable to communicate, which we'll talk about later in the book. Right now this is a sign for you to move on, not to stop your job search, but keep on looking.

In some cases you can hold on for about a year and make it work, but the aggravation of such a boss will most likely make it imperative to change companies anyway, so you may as well not waste time. I have found that companies that allow such people to move into positions of influence don't offer much in the way of long-term career advancement.

Another sign of early sandbars is when everyone who works at the place is constantly and vociferously bitching about the company. There is something wrong with the management of such places. These days, with so many microcompanies flourishing on the edge of tomorrow's profits, such places are common. The management policies are usually based on benign neglect, the pay scales iffy and the people crazed. These are good places for gaining some background and training; but they are seldom to be viewed in the long term for serious career seekers.

DO: Learn how to use such situations, sucking out the experience and training you can, then moving on quickly to more secure positions.

DON'T take backbiting, sniveling, whining or minor discomforts seriously. See them as short-term annoyances until you get what you want.

Power Packs

Early in your career you are not likely to have much in the way of power. Energy you will have; clout you can quickly gain, whether on your own talents or on someone else's piggyback. What you must develop early is a knowledge of power and how it works in a corporate situation. You must learn who the power people are in your company.

The clearest way to learn is to watch who gets what they want and who gets mad about not getting what they want. You can't always tell by the shouting, since powerful people often are crabby and not in very good moods all the time. In my first job I worked for a woman who was roundly disliked by everyone except maybe me and her boss, who happened to be the general manager of the company. Because of him she had power. She screamed and shouted at the light bulbs when they burned out, but she got every single thing she wanted. That was borrowed power, but she had it. I had borrowed clout, since I worked for her and in essence was seen to be representing her and ultimately her boss whenever I asked for things. Because I was such a sweetheart and asked nicely, I also heard the gripes about her. It was like those detective movies where the cops send in the rough guys to quiz the suspects, then send in the nice guys to get the facts. It was just a barrel of fun and I got out as soon as I landed another job eleven months later.

Later on someone negotiated the sale of her division at a wonderful profit, which gave him the ultimate power in the company, and he got rid of her and her boss, ushering in another reign of terror. Obviously, such a place offered no career advancement for a growing boy, but it was a nice place to watch power played close up.

Power usually rests with the people who are bringing in the most revenues for the company, period. Business is for making money; if you make it, you have power. At this point of the game, you must focus on building your moneymaking talents for the company, and letting your credits, salary and perks accrue. Whatever you do early in your career should be focused on creating something valuable for your company.

At this point, you should be developing a clear view of how power works, and how you will work it when you get it.

> **DO:** Remember that you are only as good as your last earnings report unless you have the support of someone very powerful.
>
> **DON'T** get the idea that because you wield a lot of power now someone else won't wield more of it over you at another time.

Pets, Mentors, Prodigies and Friends

The word "pet" has a pejorative ring to it, stemming as it does from those obnoxious ducks who were favorites of the teacher or the coach back in grade school or high school. Well, school is a preamble to "real" life, especially whenever you discover bosses and employees. People develop favorites and tend to show them special consideration in a corporate situation. The recipients of such attentions can benefit or not benefit from the game plan, depending on how it's played.

The best situation is to be a general favorite, to have everyone wish you well because you're just so beamish and talented and all. The only time I ever saw that happen was the night Michael Jackson swept the Grammies, and then we weren't too sure about some of the losers' true feelings. In general, pets and prodigies have as much resentment to contend with as they have favoritism.

Usually the pet is the special favorite of one person who may or may not be a mentor of the pet. The basic rule is that even if you do become a pet of one or more influential people, it is best not to tie your loyalties to any one person. You must somehow manage to maintain your independence so that you can move around in your career as you see fit.

The situation is very difficult. How do you accept graciously the help and attendant clout of having an influential exec take an interest in your career? How can you accept advice, direction, and even the aid of his or her clout to back up your projects without becoming an extension of his or her career? And to complicate matters you will most likely feel a genuine liking and loyalty for the person who has so kindly extended a helping hand out of what seems the generosity of his or her heart.

The first approach is not to address the problem directly. Make lots of friends besides the mentor. While forging your friendship with the sponsor make friends with other people on your own level. You should also use your clout as a pet to meet other influential execs. Do your mentor proud by extending charm and modesty—putting your best foot forward—so others will also share the desire to help you.

Too many pets or prodigies tend to become like spoiled cats, feeling they can get away with being somewhat difficult or temperamental because the mentor is carrying the load for them. Never increase your mentor's load; use the situation to prove that his trust in you is warranted and thus give credence to his judgment. By being charming and conscientious and by focusing on doing your projects as brilliantly as possible, you are paying back your debt as pet, and enhancing both your reputations.

Example: When your mentor has gone out on a limb to back you up and get certain projects for you, you must focus on the work. Never overstep yourself by assuming that you have totally arrived with the biggies just because you may have sudden access to them via your mentor. Maintain the attitudes and decorum—the modesty, as it were—usually expected of someone of your level. Express your talents, not your ego. Defer to the higher-ups; show respect for their ideas. Use the time to ask for advice from them, and don't rely totally on the advice of your mentor. By doing this, you will extend your clout and subtly make it clear that you are not locked into anyone. It makes it clear that you are accepting honest help and utilizing it correctly, but that you are still an independent entity.

This is necessary especially since your mentor's rivals may try to work against him by aiming their barbs against you. By subtly fuzzing the issue about whether or not you really are a pet, you can keep both of you safe and secure.

Pets often tend to disregard the importance of good relationships with the peers and co-workers. You are all starting out and you are the one getting the attention. Remember, if you will, that some people are early starters, others are late. Some people pull their act together when faced with the added competition. Make friends with the people who are at your level. Evaluate them and their future possibilities. Don't make enemies of any of them just because one or two may seem to exhibit no early fire. Every dog has his day—even dogs—and you never know who may be able to help or harm you later on down the shooting gallery.

You can't tread too carefully when you are a pet, so remember these things:

DO: Be careful how closely involved you become with a mentor. Do keep a low profile until you see the reactions to your being a pet. Prove that any special favors you get are warranted. Work harder than people who are not pets. Use the opportunity to advance yourself, to express your best ideas, to get more money. Take on assignments, and exhibit initiative of your own —not just as an imitation of your mentor's style. Develop your own style. Ask for things like better office space, perks and considerations, since such visible proofs of your clout lock it in. Once the company commits itself to you, it is more likely to keep backing you up to prove it was right. Do allow your clout to build gradually, even though you are given this or that plum assignment and are bringing in this or that much revenue.

DON'T forgo the trappings of petdom out of some sense of false modesty; these things are part of the tangibles of business success and increase your reputation. Don't allow yourself to be glamorized and swept into a sort of exclusive relationship. It helps to keep people at all levels on your side.

Pros and Cons

Despite the pitfalls, the mentor–protégé relationship is respected in business when it is played out correctly. The protégé may not actually be a pet in every instance; it may be that the mentor has found a valuable employee and decides to focus on developing the person's talents so that he himself will have a superdependable colleague. And the protégé or pet has an invaluable opportunity to learn the business and grow in it.

A problem develops when the protégé decides that this isn't exactly what he or she wants out of life after all and opts for a move into another area of the business. This often leaves the mentor feeling angry and betrayed. One must guard against this kind of reaction. At no time in business should any boss lay this kind of reaction on a protégé. Assumedly the mentor received a good staff member for the length of time the person was with him. Nobody owns anybody else in business, and the mentor must not allow emotional reactions or vindictiveness to shadow his protégé's decision to depart.

On the other hand, a mentor may create a monster. The protégé may not be as talented as the mentor believes; in fact, without the mentor the protégé may be pretty mediocre. Still the mentor, because of the commitment, emotionally and professionally clings to his protégé, gets promotions for him and generally stuffs the protégé down the company's throat despite the obvious flaws. My favorite example of this was a young woman who was such a protégée. She was so difficult to work with that metallurgists would come just to study her nickel plating, and a roller-skate company asked if they could name their wheels after her. Her mentor was everyone's idea of a Mr. Great Guy. Usually his judgment was clear, but somewhere along the line he became convinced that this woman was the next Clare Boothe Luce. He spent probably half his time arbitrating her battles, since if she didn't get her way every step of the way she would storm into his office and demand that he get it for her. Her career survived his resignation from the company by exactly two months.

The Rest of Us

Some of us are stars, God love us, and the rest of us, frankly, just aren't that hot. This does not mean that less spectacular people are less talented or even less valuable, just that they must take a different approach. No successful business person can deny that fate sometimes takes a hand in the affairs of corporate successions, that sometimes people who are seemingly undeserving become internationally famous, and that some damn good talents have to struggle for every damn penny they get.

The thing you must do at the start of your career—or do now, if you've been dragging your feet—is to take realistic stock of yourself, of the kind of effect you have on people, and plan your strategy accordingly. If you have always been class president, obviously you have some effect on people that makes them trust you with leadership. If you have always had to study about three hours a night more than your buddies who were making the same or better grades, then bear in mind that you'll probably have the same patterns to deal with in a job situation.

If you are a star, don't think you never have to produce something valuable to stay on top. If you are a workhorse, don't waste time resenting people who seem to have it made. You can get to the same place using more than one method.

CHAPTER **3**

Moving Up

"It doesn't matter if you work hard, as long as you work smart."

EARLY IN YOUR career you will have to become familiar with two basic areas: power and how it works; and how to read the signals about when and where to move next. As we said in the previous chapter, you can always tell who has power in your company by watching to see who gets what he wants. The reason for becoming aware of these people is pretty obvious: you won't want to make enemies of power people.

There is another factor at work here as well. Do you want to play the kinds of games your company demands to gain power there? Or do you want to play your own game of moving up? Do you want to keep your self-respect, or do you figure that success is the ultimate human condition?

Indecision becomes a factor early in anyone's career. Some people wonder if they should claw and bite to get ahead; others wonder only who should be clawed and bitten. Since no one argues with success in the corporate world—or anywhere else, for that matter—certain kinds of underhanded practices can be seen as viable alternatives for people whose creative talents are less defined than their political acumen.

Other types of indecision also crop up. How do you handle your first big crisis? How do you read the signals to move on past that first plateau? Are you ready for the first big promotion? How do you keep your head when all the people around you are losing theirs? When do you sit tight and when do you brazenly forge ahead?

The Basis of Power

In a simplistic way corporate power is based on money. The people who have power are the ones who can generate revenues for the company—or the ones the company thinks can generate revenues. That's the heart of the matter. Now, there are currently lots of young people in companies who generate revenues, who make salaries in six or near-six figures, and who don't have power. This is because they don't know how to use the stuff. Having the base of power is one thing; being able to build on that base, to get people behind you, to develop the wisdom to utilize these loyalties for meaningful corporate decisions—that's something else again.

When I was in one position, trembling on the brink of a career there, I noticed there was one officer of the company who had no discernible function, although he wielded power and was someone to be acknowledged. After puzzling it out for a few weeks I finally closed the door of my boss's office and asked why someone of such apparent, shall we say, stupidity was so important to the company. What was not readily apparent to the camera's eye?

My boss confided that this man was the company pimp, pure and simple. For the past twenty years or so he had been procuring ladies of the evening for afternoon trysts with the geriatrics who ran the place. That was his job, the basis of his power and his whole function, except when he'd come in and ask some question that no one understood.

Such a story has mostly entertainment value, since the man didn't have much interest in who was moving up from the younger ranks and he posed no threat to anyone's career. Nonetheless it would have been bad policy to adopt an offhand or scornful manner with such a person, since he came from a generation of corporate thinking that made his a very valuable function in the company. The point is that anyone who has power must be accommodated, at least cordially. He may not have cared to stand in anyone's way, but he certainly had the ability to do so if his dander was aroused. And for a man such as he, aroused dander was his stock in trade.

These days there are almost no single power figures left on the corporate scene. People such as Howard Hughes, J. Paul Getty—these mogul types are not extant. Power in companies is more or less a shared thing, for several reasons. The primary reason is that with the economy acting like a spaceship out of control, no one person has all the answers. Another equally valid reason is that with government interference so prevalent, no one can afford to be in the position of accepting the blame. Even the Mob sort of blurs its big shots these days. Nowadays power in business is based on the strength of the company as a whole, and more people can share its rewards.

It's important to remember that fact as you segue into more important levels of executive sway, since the exercises of power are less defined, less simplistic and more dependent on cooperative attitudes. In the old days there was one big shot with the power, and all the other company people squabbled with one another vying for his favor so that they could get him to use his power to their advantage. Now everyone has some sort of power, yet no one person seems to have ultimate power. Everyone has to talk and cooperate and share the clout.

If all this sounds undefined, it's because it is. Power is a tangible only when you're hit with it. The rest of the time it sleeps there, as if in a battery, waiting for someone to flick the switch.

Go on the idea that power gained early might be lost. Example: A young woman in a company was responsible for generating some $2.3 million of revenue for her company. She could have anything she wanted. What she wanted was to scream, yell and make life perfectly miserable for everyone, whether they were for her or not. Her bosses forbore to reprimand her while she was generating revenue. But then the economy put her on the slide for a while, and suddenly there was talk of easing her out. Then no one would talk to her, she wasn't privy to important executive chitchat, and no one had anything good to say for her. Eventually she became a minor executive and had to leave the company. She had failed to do anything except squander her power on temporary ego gratification. They'll always get you for that.

When to Make the Move to Move

How do you know when you are ready to make a move upward in the company? Quite simply, you know by what's going on in your head. One successful executive put it this way: "The basic indicator is that you're antsy and bored and you're repeating the same old stuff over and over again. You need a change."

That's how you know when *you're* ready; but how do you know when something is ready for you? Just plain grumpiness isn't going to generate a promotion and a raise.

When you feel this way you must talk to someone about it—someone who can effect the change. First you must take stock of what your dissatisfactions are and have concrete complaints and alternative suggestions to provide. List your assets—more for your self-confidence, to show that you have been doing a lot of the things you want to do officially—then go talk from a secure vantage point.

When I wanted my first promotion—and it was evident no one was going to give it to me, since I was already doing the job without the title and the money—I went in to my boss, sat down and asked for it point-blank. It was a nice scene. He was caught off guard a little and wasn't really prepared to go through the ritual of making such a major change. I made it clear that I wasn't going to take no for an answer, and within a week I was doing what I had been doing all along, except now I had the money and the position.

The reason I chose that time to make the move was that my boss was in a state of disarray. He was too busy to think about finding someone else for the job. A year before I had been too inexperienced for it, and the person who was there had left in disgrace, which reflected badly on my boss. If I had waited for him to pull his act together and look outside, I would have been stuck for years with no movement, since such positions were rare in my area. It is important to choose the optimum time to go in and pick the apple. In my case, there wasn't much choice for him: I was doing the job despite his reservations about wanting to promote me; if I stopped doing the job, he would be truly inconvenienced. Because of the way the company was set up, I could even have used his state of disarray to go around him and get the job anyway, which would have been one short step to getting his. (I wasn't ready to take his, unfortunately.)

Essentially, he had to say yes, and since the company was on him to find someone, and they knew me, I got it. Remember: the person who moves up is not the one who spends time wondering, Should I go ask for the job? It is important to make your move swiftly when the time is right.

DO: Take advantage of being at the right time at the right place. Make sure the people in charge hear about your abilities, even if you have to tell them.

DON'T be a shy-ris. If a promotion is sitting there waiting for someone to fill it, fill it—be aggressive!

Signs of Times to Move

There are several instances when it should be clear to you as a perceptive young exec that it's time for you to move up or move out. Following are some of these situations.

• A VACANCY OCCURS in a position that you either want to fill or are one of the people who should be considered to fill. At this time you must list your areas of expertise, make a compilation of reasons why you are best for the job, and present your case to whoever is making the decision.

• THE COMPANY IS in a state of upheaval, either because of a merger or because of a reorganization. Everyone is sitting waiting for the ax to fall and hoping it won't be he. You do not engage in such foolishness. You are not a rabbit in the woods running from the fire. You look around quickly at the executives who are calm, and decide which areas are essential. You align yourself with the people in those areas and get yourself transferred. When the dust settles you get more money and a better title. Because you survived, you will have much more power.

• THERE IS A JOB or a department that the company needs, but at the moment it is not in existence. You define a job for yourself and even set up a plan for a new department, and present it to the company. We will discuss the specifics of this later in the book.

• SOME HIGHER-UP REALIZES that there is something missing and mentions it to you. You start putting ideas together to show the feasibility of creating the new job for yourself.

• YOU ARE ONE of several people who should be next in line for a vacated position—perhaps your boss has departed, bless his hide. Everyone is talking about who the most logical successor will be. You know who it should be, so you don't indulge in discussions that bring up other people's good points. You hold firm, become superdependable, superconservative and supervisible. You take one hour only for lunch. You don't whine. You provide an opportunity for the decision-maker to talk to you about the position.

Now, there may be the problem that you just don't have the experience for the job. In that case you do the same things, only you keep quiet, hold firm and gravitate to the most likely winners. When the choice is made you extend a sincere congratulations and reaffirm your loyalty to the new boss. And become very visible to that person.

DO: Listen to all gossip around the office pertaining to changes that are imminent.

DON'T say anything about what you know.

Upheavals

While being in the right place at the right time can be a matter of dumb luck, one must possess a certain insight. Many people see the situation but do not have the savvy to act, and they spend their careers waiting for the next go-round. To be able to act decisively you must not moralize, but must act directly and with intelligence.

One young woman executive told us of her own "luck" in this matter. Her company was about to merge with a larger one. Some departments were to be phased out in the merger, and a transition team was to be kept on as part of the new company. "I had a passing acquaintance with a woman exec in another department, which covered the area I had been wanting to get into. On the day the merger was announced, I realized that I could equivocate no longer; I went and asked her for a job in her department which I thought would not be phased out. My previous boss was pushed out, and my new boss and I were kept on as part of the transition team."

She added this interesting sidelight: "Word got out, and people were suddenly following me around because of my link with the woman, who suddenly was in a position of power. It was almost an unconscious reaction. Wherever I'd go I'd suddenly find myself the focus of attention."

Mergers are good times for power plays of this sort and provide as much opportunity to move up as to be phased out. We were told of one astute male executive who always made it his business to know what was happening in the company so that he could predict what the next move should be. He was able to find out first about his company's merger, and placed himself in the front line of the transition team. For a while people actually stood when he entered a room.

> **DO:** Dig for information in discreet ways.
>
> **DON'T** tell anything to anyone unless you are imparting a fact to gain more information from someone you know can be opened up.
>
> **DON'T** indulge in conversation on a casual basis, except to listen.

Knowing Secrets

Power sometimes is based on knowing where the bodies are buried. One female executive, now retired from the fray, gained a great deal of power in her industry through using her brains and guts in this way. "I was called at home one Sunday evening around eleven-thirty and was told to come into the office immediately. I told them I was about to go to bed. They told me to get down there right away or else.

"I got down to the office, and there were security men all over the place. One of the executives was taking over and pushing out another one who was over me. There was some kind of illegality and nefariousness involved—I'm not clear about all the details now. I was called in and told to hand over a bunch of documents, and I refused. I managed to get a promise of a promotion and a lot more money, and all the next week I watched as people were called in and axed, called in and axed, including the man who was over me. I just stood my ground. I knew I had something that was needed, and I wasn't about to let it go without getting something equally big for it. You can't ever let yourself be beaten down by threats. You have to know what your power is and what it's worth.

"I watched a lot of people get axed because they were too scared to stand up. The security men were a psychological factor. What could they do to me? Or anybody? They weren't government agents, and I hadn't committed a crime. So I ignored them. People came crying to me for help after they were fired, but at that time there wasn't anything to be done."

When Nasties Succeed

There are so many wonderful clichés to say that every dog has his day, and it would be even nicer if such were always the case. The business world is full of nasty and incompetent people who nevertheless manage to gain positions of power through sheer determination, one-shot talents, sex and/or guts. This is not to imply that everyone makes it through nastiness, but there are enough of these success stories to give one pause. It is also true that in most cases these people eventually get moved out, though never soon enough to make much of a difference to the people who have had to put up with them over a period of years, or who have had their careers hurt because of them.

What can be done about them? Not much. They often get there by being nice to the proper people in some way, then are kept there partly because it's easier than getting rid of them, and partly because nobody wants to admit that he was responsible for letting them stay so long. Laziness on the part of higher-ups accounts for much of these occurrences. They just don't want to deal with the problem; it's easier to ignore the person, to justify his existence, to accept his excuses, to let him pretend that others are at fault and let him fire this or that scapegoat.

Finally someone gets to the point of having had enough of it and takes the final step and ousts the person. And everyone says, "At last they caught onto him!" But of course by this time a lot of people have suffered. One reason the corporate structure can support these people in such style is that there are so many people who want to work under any circumstances and these are the ones who make things go. This provides an opportunity for these Peter Principle types to rise even higher. They are in a sense being given less work to do so that they can spend even more time making inroads, plotting assassinations, and making themselves look good by taking credit for the work of others.

People who get ahead through sex generally don't last as long as other types of undesirables. Those who utilize the slaughterhouse method of staying in power often may run into reversals of fortune, too, some of which can be amusing. One young female exec who fit into both slots and who had risen into the six-figure salary ranks rather earlier than her talents should have warranted was reported worried because her protector at the company was marrying a woman she had fired.

"If you wait long enough," the remark was made by yet another woman who was also brutally fired, "something always happens—but who wants to wait?"

DO: Find ways to shut out the nasties whenever the opportunity arises. Don't kid yourself that you can woo them where no one else has succeeded. Too often they will do what they can to terminate the very people who have courted them. The old viper-in-the-bosom syndrome.

DON'T do charity work at the office. If a person is psychologically unable to deal with people on a fair, realistic basis, it is not up to you to squander your professional energies bringing him around. Vicious people should be eliminated from the company whenever possible, and allowed to seek help when they come to the realization that their rotten tactics aren't succeeding. If their rotten tactics are allowed to succeed, don't blame them if you've helped them get ahead.

Dirty Tricks

Since Watergate, dirty tricks are much more in evidence in all walks of life, and that includes corporate affairs. It is amazing how seamy and sordid some of the machinations are behind the scenes of our glamorous and sophisticated corporations. It's a shame that so many of them succeed, thus lowering the general quality of sources for future promotion, and forcing many otherwise honest people to have to make a choice of either raiding the compost pile or working for someone who has done so.

It's also a shame that so many talented people suffer from a crippling insecurity and indulge in such practices on a regular basis. Some dirty tricks—in fact, most of them—imitate childhood practices. Others are more complex, reflecting the mind of an unfair or oftentimes sick adult. Here are some of them:

• TALEBEARERS. My own personal favorite, since it seems that such a juvenile practice is too obvious to work—and then it works. Usually it's evidenced in a person who uses charm to make friends and gain trust among co-workers, then goes behind their backs to tell the boss all negative gossip. People should refuse to work with him or to discuss projects in his presence. In general shut him out.

If he makes up lies to retaliate, co-workers can organize and demand that the boss oust him. Depending on the quality of the boss in the first place, people like this often move up despite their evil ways. Unless there is a concerted effort to eliminate them before they gain power, it becomes too late after they are ensconced in administrative positions. Take a tip from the gardeners: nip certain flowers in the bud to strengthen the whole plant.

• UPPER-LEVEL JUNKIES. One high-ranking executive had a problem—drug problems, actually—that made her a candidate for retirement, ouster or the loony bin. Unfortunately, she was kept on and everyone under her kept being fired, since the president of the company had a strong loyalty toward her. She blamed everyone under her for her mistakes, discredited people, fired them, and still she was maintained.

Solution: Take the money and run. Demand a high pay at the start when going to work under such people, then cope. Use the position as a bargaining tool to get a better job elsewhere—either in the same company or in another one.

• GOSSIP. Telling anything about anyone that reflects badly on his or her character is a dirty trick, even if the gossip is true. Basically everyone has some dead body somewhere, but whose business is it? Gossip is a harmful tool. Even when it is true or the gossip is innocuous, it casts a seemingly sordid light over the person being discussed, and can damage a reputation. The very fact that someone is saying something at all negative about an absent person casts a shadow over that person.

Solution: There is no real antidote for gossip, except never to engage in it or take what you hear too seriously. Listen, don't speak.

Someone who has made a career of gossiping and backstabbing will often find himself out of a job. I know of one man who spent his best energies backstabbing, lying, talebearing, gossiping and what all, and after eight years found himself with an expensive co-op apartment, huge expenses, no job, and a reputation that was so foul no one wanted to hire him.

• SECRET ENEMIES. These are the ones who pretend to be working for you so that they can get things from you—even loyalty—while working to discredit you behind the scenes. These people will even blame others for their own actions against you, to whitewash themselves.

Solution: Roll over them. Refuse to cooperate with them. Give them much of their own medicine, since such people usually do to others exactly that which they're afraid will be done to them. Don't ever trust them about anything.

There are many kinds of dirty tricks that people can use. In all cases it is best to be friends with everyone you work with, while maintaining a clear picture of who your enemies are.

DO: Keep your enemies in plain sight. An old Roman saying is, keep your enemies close, because you know what your friends are up to.

DON'T ever trust someone who has worked against you. If he gets away with it once, he'll make a practice of it.

Is It All Pol?

One may think that business is all politics. Not so: much of it is creative and satisfying work. The problems we've delineated above arise because so many people don't trust their talents, or don't like to work, so they resort to politics and subterfuge.

It is essential to develop a sense of how people behave in a work situation and have that as a tool for interaction. It is ridiculous to think that there is any human relationship that does not require a political effort to be maintained on a successful level. Much of what we call corporate affairs are an intangible kind of psychological interplay. Many people think that this is hogwash, that plain old work should be the only consideration. This is patently not true.

Business is human interaction. If we were doing it just to sell stuff to one another, we could do it with robots and spend the week at the shore. Business should be used as a tool for self-development as much as to make money. The problem we currently have is that people have lost sight of that aspect.

In the first part of this chapter we have tried to set forth the psychology of moving up, and to show that you can get ahead by solving problems on a creative basis—not having to resort to taking the low road. This requires a constant self-evaluation, as we said earlier also, so that you can develop the kind of security that enables you to move up on your merits and not on the crushed careers of others.

The second part of this chapter is based on methods rather than thought processes. The same judgment must be used to select the proper methods for your own advancement and to figure out people and how they function.

Moving Again

There is no hard-and-fast rule about the number of years an executive must remain at a particular company. Usually that is determined by your effectiveness on the job, both in your own judgment and in that of your employers. Some areas require short tenures because of the nature of the projects the company is involved in. Some companies like people to stay around forever, even past the point where they lose effectiveness. There are companies that hate to let go, just as there are executives who hate to give up favorite jobs.

It is difficult to imagine anyone outgrowing a job within a year, unless the company is just an impossible place to work in. But if your career is stagnating after that time, start looking around. Don't get locked in to certain considerations, such as glamor, ease of work, pleasant atmosphere or company prestige. Often such things are a drain on your energies, and you can become lazy and stop putting out effort to keep your talents honed.

NOTE: It has been observed that conservative companies which utilize long-term projects are relatively free of the backstabbing and the competitive pressures visible in high-changeover companies. This is because the needs of such conservative companies are specific and based on particular talents and skills that are untainted, as it were, by political chicanery. People tend to be fairly stationary and are content to pursue creative satisfaction rather than having to claw for power. In a more mutable business, cutthroat tactics tend to be used to hang on to whatever one has built up; infighting too often becomes the rule as people must constantly show themselves to be equal to the changes that constantly occur in the company. When stress gets to be too much, biting and clawing occur.

Hunters of Heads

When you're in business there is always that wish to be sought after for jobs, to have employment agencies know who you are and call you about a hot new opening. The usual fantasy is that right after your fourth disagreement with your boss you are sitting contemplating a dramatic resignation, when the phone rings. It is a head hunter. Of course he knows of you and is aware that you are "unhappy with your present position," since it is all over town that you are not appreciated where you are. He has several important biggies at Exxon who have only been waiting for a signal from you before they move to woo you away to that big office in the sky. . . . Well, anyway, that's the fantasy.

First, remember that we are in a funny economy and that head hunters have to eat just like the rest of the cannibals. They make it their business to seek out companies where there are openings, then make a simultaneous search for bodies very often at companies with employee-training programs. For a fee, they will try to slot you into those openings. It doesn't mean you are the sudden star of your area without being aware of it. It only means someone got your name from someone. Don't jump at the chance.

Your first reaction should be to thank the recruiter and ask if you can call back. Don't be rushed. If the recruiter tries to pressure you, make it clear that you need more information before committing yourself to an interview. Ask where he or she got your name. Then call that person and ask something about the head hunter. Is he reputable or worthy of the name Hunter of Heads for Big Bucks? Do not send your resumé to this caller until you have information on him and then insist on a personal meeting where you will make your decision whether or not to be represented by this agency. Once they have your resumé, what is to keep them from sending out copies of it to every company in creation? It does not reflect well on you to have your resumé active in this shotgun manner. It is best to appear selective.

You must determine whether or not the agent is coming to you with a bona fide opening or is just scouting. Even if there is a job opening, does the head hunter "have" the job, or is he just trying to get someone he can present to the company? You can do that yourself. Very often the head hunter has no more clout than you do, and, rather than you being sought, the situation turns around to you being the seeker, when all you did was answer your phone. Ask this question very directly and succinctly of the agent: Did this company come to him looking for an executive, and is he already in touch with the company—more specifically, with the management people who will make the decision on hiring?

When judging an agency, note these things: Is their secretary a real pro, or is she fairly casual about you, sort of as though you're just another steer passing through the gates? If you have made an appointment and have brought your resumé, does she hand you a basic application to fill out? At a certain point it is annoying to think anyone would care where you went to grade school, and more annoying to have to write out all the information that is already on your resumé. Does the secretary know who you are when you call back, or does she ask you every time who you are and if you've ever been there before? It should not be too much to ask that your name be remembered by the folks at your personnel agency.

DO: Stay calm and sober when approached by a head hunter. Their jobs entail painting gold paint over everything. Make sure you should be looking for a job at all at this time in your career.

DO: Ask your search firm to give you two references of executives they have placed, so that you can check out how they were treated and what their satisfactions and complaints were.

DON'T take it for granted that you are ready to move just because something new is available. One assumes you want to make the best use of your efforts and don't want to throw it all away to run off with a head hunter. Evaluate your experience and your reputation, then say yes or no.

Keeping It a Secret

It becomes a touchy business to keep your search for a new job secret from your present employer. If you have a strong enough resumé, however, you should be able to stand on your experience without the aid of current references to get you a job. People tend to hire on the basis of interviews and gut feelings as much as on past experience. If you are high-powered enough, it is as likely you will be sought out by avid head hunters as you are searching.

At lower levels, you must decide if your boss should know you are looking for a new job. A boss may either accommodate the search, adjust the present job to make it more to your liking, or just wish you well. Or tell you to go to hell; which is something you must be prepared for always.

Reputable search firms for executives are possibly the best way to look around in certain professions, particularly if your search needs a real camouflage. The problem is that you are limited to their sources. You must be very careful here, as there have been horror stories of resumés being mass-mailed and turning up on the desk of one's own employer. Always demand that you be consulted before the resumé is sent out. Often the head hunter doesn't want you to know the company for fear you'll go off on your own. You must maintain a sense of honor here. Very often the search firm's sources are no better than your own, and a company may not consider you if they have to pay a fee to get you.

There is always a danger that a friend of your boss may gain access to the resumé and inform him of your search. This may work for or against you, depending on how badly your boss wants to keep you. There are some companies who still let executives go based on the fact that they are looking for jobs.

DO: Be courteous when being courted by a search firm. Give them their space in case they are the genuine article. They will help you to know at any given point in your career whether or not you are a marketable executive. But it's also important to know whether or not you are at the right point to be marketed. If you are satisfied with the way your career is going, and are getting the right money and credit and clout, it may be best to build up a stronger base where you are. It is just as impressive to refuse an interview as it is to be courted by a prestigious company.

DON'T allow your name to be sent out to companies you don't know. Don't answer blind ads.

Don't allow yourself to be bullied or danced around by head hunters. Don't fool around with any searcher or company that acts in any way less than what you consider a professional manner.

Other Considerations

Always bear in mind that there is seldom, if ever, such a thing as a once-in-a-lifetime opportunity. If you operate on such a philosophy, then you should reflect on your maturity and development and perhaps seek ways to improve them. If a job offer comes your way, and you are unable or unwilling to accept it, you must go on the knowledge that there will be others down the road. A career is not composed of one-time-only job offers, like some discount stereo house, but of serious personal achievement and wise job choices through the years.

You must always take the long view when considering job possibilities. You should accept job interviews or seek them only when it is clear that you are ready to make a change, or when you know that an outside offer may strengthen your bargaining position at your present job.

You should not maintain an active status with an employment agency. It is assumed that you want to work part of the time, not just jump from triumph to triumph. It is politically essential to display an aloofness part of the time. This will help you weed out false leads, since the search firm will call you only when there is a real opportunity you should look into. It is never attractive to salivate over dream jobs. Use your time spent at any given job to build your reputation, increase your circle of friends, and network yourself so that you have a solid reputation behind you.

Very often moving from a smaller firm to an equal or similar position in a larger and better company will bring your salary more into the range it should be. It is not good to become too overpriced, but there is no great advantage to being underpaid either. In their ways, each situation hinders you in some way. The overpaid executive may find himself unable to move around anymore; the underpaid person may not be considered prime material for the better jobs, and may have a harder time making the larger jump into a more equitable bracket. It is usually the case that an underpaid exec should make the move as soon as possible into a position where he receives normal compensation for his level, otherwise he will be classified as a lower-quality commodity.

DO: Hold out for fair and proper compensation before accepting any new position. If you sell yourself short at the start these same people will continue to take advantage of you throughout your stay with the company. If you do not have the self-confidence to do this, you must steel yourself to find the guts to do so. In general it is always better to view financial compensation as part of the business deal, and to hold out for it unless something viable is offered as a substitute.

DON'T let stressful situations of temporary duration send you packing off to the head hunter. Every job has its drawbacks. View unpleasant situations as times to hone your diplomatic and managerial skills. Figure how to turn problems and crises to your own advantage. The person who knows that every problem has a solution is the one who moves up, gains power and selects the job he will take. Don't linger over regrets about jobs passed by.

When You Want to Move

It may happen that there is nothing for you to move up to in your own company. It may be that you are with a bad company, one where your incentive and skills never receive proper recompense, no matter what you do. Some people see these situations as challenges; others prefer to work in a more benevolent atmosphere. This latter is in fact a valid consideration when deciding to change companies.

When planning to move, it is best to take steps that will enable you to receive professional advice along the way. If you have no friends to talk to in your area, or if you have no affiliation with a professional society, then you should find a reliable search firm and discuss your prospects with them. Certain professions, of course, find it easy to locate tempting job opportunities through the classified- and business-ad pages; others must rely on search-and-destroy methods, since jobs at their level are at a lower profile.

One should try to avoid answering blind ads. It is always best to know the company you are approaching. Sometimes—not often—a company with a choice position prefers to mask itself to keep away the hordes with resumés who would besiege the reception desk. At such times, use your instinct. Compare phone numbers in ads to weed out the "jerk" head hunters who try to lure the unsuspecting into their lairs.

When answering an ad, try to follow its directions to the letter. If it says resumés only, for example, don't start wondering if that means you should send a cover letter too. Don't send anything extra when the ad specifically tries to eliminate something. Otherwise a resumé should be sent with a cover letter.

When using a search firm, you are duty bound to go with it even if it turns out you could have gotten an interview on your own. If you try to go around a head hunter after agreeing to use one, you will lose out all around, since companies respect the validity of the search firms. If you do not want to pay a fee, or if you feel that a fee paid by a company will hinder your chances, then work on your own.

The best way to do this is to contact the company you wish to "open up," either through the personnel department or through an executive there, and send a letter introducing yourself, with a resumé. Nothing else. Follow up with a phone call about a week later, and refer to your letter. Very often, if you have said you will call, you may receive a call from the contact person, inviting you to come in or expressing regret at the lack of opportunities available. Accept either statement as valid, and try again later if there is any encouragement to do so. Don't keep dunning a company or an executive for a job, or they will wonder what on earth is wrong with you.

If you belong to a professional society, you can ask around discreetly about opportunities. If you have friends in the same area, let them know through the grapevine that you are looking, or at least available. There would not normally be anything wrong with this if it got back to your own company, since gossip is gossip, and it can be denied. It may even increase your ability to improve your present situation.

DO: As we said several times already, make friends in your field. This is the best way to keep abreast of what opportunities are available, and to make yourself known.

DON'T feel you have to leave a company once you have thought about it, or even if you spark a job offer. Very often just having the freedom to move will spark your energies and make you realize you are happy with your present position after all. Don't be afraid to use a job offer as a tool to get better compensation from your present company. Don't however, go to your boss and *say,* "I have this offer, but I'll stay if you beat the price." Play it more diplomatically. Let him make the offer. If he doesn't, frankly, you're better off leaving.

Staying at a Spot

It may be that you choose to stay at a certain level of management or executive position. If so, you must realize that the money won't change dramatically even if you do move around to other companies. Salaries are generally competitive at certain levels, and the possibility of more than incremental raises is pretty slim. It is also recommended that if you choose to "sleep" in this way, you should develop some side interest that will bring in money and provide you with satisfaction. Many middle-level jobs do not sit well on older people, and you are heading toward a position of nonpower. This means, bluntly, that you can easily be fired as everyone around you and everyone above you gets younger. Eventually they will want to replace you with someone younger, someone to whom they can pay the base-level salary.

It can become embarrassing. I was told of one man who had held the same basic-level job for some fifteen years. Over the years his normal salary increments accumulated so that he was making more than one of the two people he reported to. Because of an economic crunch, the only way to get more money for his supervisor was to fire him, hire someone out of school, and split the extra freed money among the higher-ups. It was a sticky situation, but it wasn't economical to keep paying a middle-aged man a high salary for a job an entry-level person could do as well or better.

There is nothing wrong with holding a position as long as you continue to grow creatively, increase your value to the company, and remain indispensable. This kind of growth in itself is a sort of upward movement.

The Lateral Move

One does not move up every time one changes jobs. It may be that you have started out in one kind of position and find that it isn't what you want. You have a few years of solid experience and are even getting promoted. Your boss loves you and you do your job well. And you hate it. So you start looking for a way to move sideways to get a foothold in an area that pleases you more. This is fine. Sometimes—indeed, most of the time—people don't have clear-cut career goals until they see a business from the inside. This can be a chance to see more clearly where your own talents lie.

When I started out in my first job on a newspaper, I worked a split week—half in the business section, half in the entertainment section. It was a little weird going from Dow Jones to Doris Day every Wednesday, but the financial writer turned to me one day and expressed his envy. "You know, I've been trying to get a job as a movie critic for years," he said. "And I've been stuck here as a financial writer because that's where I started." I told him I wished I knew a little more about money, but it didn't make him feel good. He had awards for his writing, so over the years he had gotten stuck in a job that everyone figured he must like because he did it so admirably.

Many people feel they have to stay where they are because they are doing the work so well. It is important to be doing what you want if it is at all possible; that should be your primary consideration. It does not make any difference if you lose some financial ground for a few years if you can reestablish yourself where you want to be. As for titles, they can also be caught up with; and a higher position in one area may equal a lower position somewhere else. The important thing is to end up where you want to be, to look forward to the work facing you every morning, and to get a thrill out of the discussions pertaining to your work because you sincerely care about it.

DO: Consider job satisfaction to be part of what you want out of your career, even if there is a small sacrifice of money along the way.

DON'T make money your only reason for working.

Money Is Funny

Have you ever wondered why some people are able to negotiate large salaries when they don't have much more to offer than you, for instance, do? You may also have noticed then that someone who came much later into the company and is not a known quantity, such as you are, has somehow managed to pull down a larger compensation than you do. All of this can make a person very nervous. Do you really increase your salary if you move around often? Sometimes. It all depends on who you are, how confident you are in your talents and how desirable you have managed to make yourself to a new employer.

Generally speaking, most companies try to pay the minimum going rate for a particular job in a particular type of business. If a person can convince a company that he or she has something that will increase revenues, the company will usually be willing to pay that person more than another executive of equal or even higher standing. Moneymaking ability always pulls a higher salary. If you happen to be in a certain career that doesn't directly pull in revenue for a company, you don't have much to bargain with unless you happen to get another offer and the company happens to feel that you are worth the extra chips to keep you. Then your cultivation of goodwill comes into play. They'd rather give you the money than lose you, because they like you. Maybe.

Those of us who are not top revenue pullers can perhaps increase our normal salary brackets by about 10 percent by changing companies selectively and somewhat more frequently than usual. Otherwise the general consensus is that most companies maintain competitive salary ranges and that a person who remains in a position for a normally long period will in fact find that his or her salary level is within the going range for that position.

The most important factors affecting salary levels are usually the state of the economy, the health of your own company, and the state of business in your area. We are in a state of continual economic change, and many established businesses feel this instability. Newer companies are spread thin while waiting for the future to pay off. This instability, combined with increasing governmental latitude into your salary, taxwise, makes it necessary for you to determine your needs carefully.

DO: Approach new positions and promotions with an eye to more gradual financial rewards on a more even curve upward. Make yourself thoroughly aware of your personal market value, and consider security, prestige, future opportunity and stock options in a more important light.

DON'T, on the other hand, think that just because things are rough a company can't afford to meet your reasonable demands for more money. Many companies use the ploy of the economy to shut out raises that they can afford. Make yourself aware of when a company —especially your own—can and truly cannot afford to meet your needs.

Cooperation

The best tool for moving up is keyed in the word "cooperation." That is what working smart means. You must respect the space of other people in the company, whether they work with you, for you or above you. This does not mean being such a sap that no one can stand you. Personality is part of your image, after all. Don't become the Smiling Android of the company just to hold a position.

Remember always that everybody is there for the same reasons: to work, to move up, to gain a position where they can achieve a creative fulfillment of some sort. The executive who understands this and sees himself or herself as part of the whole package will have an easier time moving up.

CHAPTER **4**

Give a Letter, Take a Letter:

You and Your Secretary

I'd wish you a Happy Birthday, but it's not in my job description.

—INSCRIPTION ON A GREETING CARD

THE TIME COMES in most people's careers when they are finally granted a secretary or an assistant. This is the person you will be working most closely with during your business hours, and it's only fitting that we devote a chapter to the ins and outs, the do's and don'ts, of your relationship. For convenience' sake, we will use only the term "secretary," with the understanding that the same rules apply for many kinds of assistants. And, since the bulk of secretaries are women, we will refer to them as being female.

Secretaries endure—and so do their bosses who know how to deal with them. It has been very unscientifically observed that people who get along well with their secretaries don't seem to get fired, pushed out or kicked upstairs—at least until they're well past retirement age. Does this mean that the secretaries are the real heroines here? That they are really running the show? Only partly. A secretary is as good as she's allowed to be. The wise boss knows how to let his secretary flourish in the job. But that's not the key, either.

The real answer is that if a person can't learn how to build a rapport and a working relationship with his secretary, he certainly will have a bad time relating to anyone else in business. A secretary knows everything about her boss. She knows his working personality better than anyone else and sees the quirks and foibles and shams without being impressed. A secretary is the first person an executive must get along with. She works totally in concert with her boss, male or female. If the boss can't move in concert with the secretary, then he's out of sync with himself.

To set the tone for the way you want your secretary to perform, you must know what she wants and must state clearly what your needs are. If you are the type who needs a secretary to frown at you when you become strident on the phone, then that must be an agreed—not necessarily stated—factor in your office. If she does not feel comfortable serving you coffee, it must be dealt with.

Both the secretary and the boss must decide who will be the ascendant person in the office. This means knowing which of the two is cool enough to see the mistakes and guide the other one away from the pitfalls. Some bosses become rattled under pressure, and the secretary must maintain a cool head and an authoritative manner so that the boss doesn't, say, get on a plane without his tickets. Some secretaries are nervous Nellies and need to work for a more forceful type of boss who lays everything out the way he wants it. It is not important that the exec is one way or the secretary the other, only that both of them know the territory and are willing to work on the basis of the realities.

I have a friend whose secretary makes all his daytime appointments for him because she knows so well whom he wants to see, when he can or can't see them, whom he would rather avoid at certain times. When I want to have lunch with him (he is so busy that getting together with him is like playing Donkey Kong) I call her, not him, and ask when we can arrange it. Then he just magically appears at the place his secretary and I decide on.

Other executives might think this is going too far, and for them it is. But the illustration of rapport is unbeatable. This is the kind of secretary that a boss needs—someone who can *be* the boss in his absence. When he goes home, he turns into a private person again. I always found it interesting that the secretary above didn't know much about the boss's private life, unless he was going out of town, but she had a real command of his office requirements.

Reaching the right rapport with a secretary starts from the time you interview her for the job. That's where the real tone is set, and you should follow through if you want things to work out.

Hiring a Secretary

One of the roughest jobs a person has to handle is finding a secretary for the first time. If you're lucky you'll inherit a gem and you can more or less place yourself in her hands and send a check to your favorite charity in thanks or something. If you're not lucky you'll have to find one for yourself and lotsa luck, because you'll need it. Not that there aren't plenty of very good secretaries around; it's just a matter of there being so many bad secretaries mixed in with the group and you have to be perceptive enough to make a good one rise to the top.

The first problem people run into is that they don't really know what a secretary is supposed to do until they actually have one. It's amazing how many newly created executives never think to ask the young woman if she can type. Or, worse, how many just ask, "You can type, can't you?" in a sort of sardonic way, as if to say, "Of course you *do*." Later on it turns out that of course she *can't*—at least not very well, or not very fast or not very something important. It would seem just common sense to ask an unknown secretary to take a typing test and to provide proof that she can take dictation and not file all the folders beginning with "The" in the "T" drawer.

It's not just new execs who make horror-movie choices in secretaries, but also the longtime executive who has lucked out with a great secretary all through his career and suddenly loses her. He has come to take it for granted that all secretaries are like the one who was there, and, childlike, he hires the first person who asks for the job. My favorite story of this type began one day when our receptionist announced cheerily to me that she was going to improve herself so that she could get a better job. As if to illustrate her point, she had her long nails poised like a pianist over a typewriter that some unsuspecting soul had placed there. She told me there was an opening for a secretary with my publisher and she was aiming to get it. Then she glared at the page in the roller, brought down her fingers and jammed the keyboard. I smiled an indulgent smile and ankled to my office. A week later I was startled to hear her call out a greeting to me from my publisher's office. She was so happy I guess nobody told her that a barracuda very often will pose as a publisher when he's out of sardines. Within another week he was screaming at her more than speaking to her. She was as shaky as a vibrator salesman, not knowing what a triple carbon was, not knowing how to write as fast as he talked. How she lasted a full three weeks no one ever knew, but her parting words when he told her she was fired were, "Nyah, nyah, nyah!"—and that's a direct quote—then she was no more.

It all could have been avoided if the publisher had exercised common sense and asked whether she had ever been a secretary. Being something of a male chauvinist, however, he thought all women who weren't his wife or his daughter were secretaries, so maybe he never thought to ask.

DO: Rely on your personnel department, or, lacking that, utilize the services of a secretarial/clerical employment agency. Or try out a temp with the understanding it can become a permanent job if things go well.

DON'T risk your filing system on a whimsical approach to hiring.

Her Basic Training

When considering hiring a secretary, examine her office skills closely. Those include:

- Typing accuracy and speed.
- Taking dictation and a knowledge of shorthand.
- Filing and the ability to create a filing system.
- Answering the phone and fielding calls according to your needs.
- Word-processing knowledge, if your company uses computers.
- A working knowledge of what a business letter is and how to create one on her own if necessary.
- Public-relations ability. Can she get along with other people? Can she get along with you? Can she be polite when clients and colleagues become overbearing on the phone or in person? Can she cope with your own panics, anxieties and quirks?

Before you can judge the secretary, of course, you must know what your own quirks are. If you are basically crazy and always pressed for time, you should tell the applicant this at the interview. If you're the kind of boss who needs the security of his secretary in the office at 6:20 A.M. on the day he's catching an 8 A.M. flight to Dallas, you should say so. Or if you are prone to call for her to carry to you across town something that you need for a meeting, and you often do this around ten minutes to five, warn her in advance. These are the things one talks about at job interviews—or *should* talk about.

DO: Consult her references. Ask her directly what she is strongest at and weakest at in relation to her skills. You may feel "real good" about someone during an interview, but if she can't find anything after she files it, what good is the feeling?

DON'T minimize personality pluses or minuses. Someone who seems quirky can really grate on you day after day. Someone who has a special "up" personality can be a big help to your own mood as well as engender a positive attitude toward you from people she deals with.

Male Secretaries

Should you hire a male secretary? These days there is still a basic prejudice against hiring a man in this kind of job. Most female execs prefer to have women working for them. Many female execs say they would hire a man if he were gay, but they would have a problem dealing with a straight man in that position. Male execs often do not care what sex the secretary is as long as the job gets done; other male execs like the atmosphere that a female brings to the job. It is still true that people are surprised to hear a male voice on the other end of the line when they call someone's office and expect a secretary. There is less prejudice against male receptionists. When you are faced with this decision, remember only who you are and what you want a secretary to do. If you can relate better to a female, then that should be your choice. If it makes no difference to you, then hire the best performer.

There does not seem to be much of a trend right now for men to go into these jobs. But as we move ahead in our society, there will probably be a blurring of prejudices and attitudes about which sex does what job in what company.

DO: Think about the effect a male secretary will have on people you deal with. Depending on the man you hire, it can come across as either superdignified or sexually suspect. If public relations isn't that important to you, then this is not a consideration. If your secretary will have to deal with clients as much as you do, decide whether or not a male might not provide the style and panache you want.

DON'T, if you are a woman exec, automatically dismiss the idea of having a male secretary. Many women do, but often the man can balance a woman executive's act. Be sure the male secretary conforms to the same standards of dress you might expect from a female. Many male secretaries don't think the suit-and-tie dress code applies to them; it does.

College Knowledge

You should pay attention to the educational background of your secretary, especially if you plan to move ahead to the top of the corporate heap. A college-educated woman may be more of an asset to you than one who is not. She may exhibit more maturity and poise and be better able to complete your image as a top-notch exec. This is not to say that someone who does not have a college degree should be passed over. An education is only as good as the intelligence and awareness of the person who received it. These days, however, any extra training seems to be desirable. On the other hand, a college graduate may not be satisfied spending all her days as a secretary and may opt for extra prestige and money. There is nothing that muddies the coffee in the morning like a disgruntled secretary who wants some other career.

Remember, too, that a person who has opted for secretarial training may be more disposed intellectually to like the career and want to stay with it. When interviewing, ask point-blank what her goals are: does she want to move up as a secretary, or does she want to use the job as a way to move into something else? You have a right to know.

DO: Provide the incentives for a secretary to work for you if she has more education. Try to offer money and benefits as befits her degree. She is bringing you more, so you should in fairness give her more.

DON'T demand more education than she'll need. You may not need a secretary who has the background of a college grad. If your secretary is going to be focused on clerical skills, you may do best with someone who has focused on secretarial training. If you need a super-aware, well-spoken publicity woman as well as a secretary, then you should seek out someone who has either the style or the education to carry out these duties.

Her Taste Level

Extracurricular activities are always indicators of the kind of person you are interviewing. There is an organization called Professional Secretaries International, and just as membership in any professional group indicates interest in one's career, membership in this or similar groups shows that your applicant means business about her career. If the woman applying also takes on such things as being a Girl Scout leader, or teaches kids things like martial (not marital) arts in her free time, you probably are looking at a very high-energy secretary who can handle a high-pressure situation for you.

A secretary's appearance will be important to you if you have a lot of influential people visiting your office. The applicant's clothes should be considered at the interview. If she's wearing pants of any kind, you should discuss the matter with her, since this is not always a fully acceptable business outfit. It may be all right on some days for a secretary to wear slacks or jeans to the office, but in general her clothes should enable her to go anywhere in the company without drawing disapproval. If she doesn't have this awareness at an interview you may have a problem. Equal-employment-opportunity laws make it illegal to discriminate against an applicant on the basis of dress. If you are going to broach the subject, it must be roundabout.

Perhaps the best way is to say, "On certain occasions—probably on most occasions here—it would work against me if my secretary were dressed in casual clothes. Would you be comfortable in this kind of situation or would you prefer to work in a place where it made no difference?" Do not make her clothes the pivotal factor about whether or not she gets the job, but open the matter to discussion to find out how she plans to look when she shows up for work.

Q & A

There are certain questions you should not ask an applicant at an interview, questions too personal to delve into which won't affect her performance on the job. Others should be asked, as they may provide the keys to the two of you working well together. Examples:

• ALTHOUGH IT IS all right to ask about hobbies, or about organizations and clubs the applicant belongs to, it is off limits to ask what she does on Saturday night for fun. You can ask whether she's married, but not whether she dates often or whether she has a boyfriend. This has nothing to do with your evaluation of her as a possible secretary.

• DON'T ASK ABOUT her family commitments, unless she brings up the subject. You assume that if she is looking for a job she will handle her commitment to her employer and balance that with her responsibilities to her family without invading your needs. If she does offer information and asks for special consideration, you can judge whether or not you want to accommodate her. It should be noted that the best secretaries manage their private lives while operating fully in the office. It may reflect badly on you if your secretary is taking a lot of time off on a regular basis to tend to her family affairs. It's best *not* to give office time off for such needs.

• YOU CAN ASK the applicant how she performs under pressure. You know how much stress you must cope with during the workday; your secretary will have to cope with exactly as much as you do, since her job, essentially, is your job. Don't try to soften the picture. Let the person know at the start whether or not she's applying for a job that some people would consider a nightmare. Remember, you are looking for someone to help you; you aren't doing charity work here.

• MAKING COFFEE. A lot of secretaries percolate at the thought of having to brew up the caffeine every morning. You may want a pot going in the office, and you may make lousy coffee. Ask her at the start if she will do it, or if she will share the task, or give it a trial period. Remember that this chore, seemingly meaningless to you, is one rallying point of complaint among secretaries. One executive secretary we spoke to said her boss asked her if she would make coffee when he interviewed her. "Like a jackass I said, 'I make great coffee!' And I've been stuck doing it for five years."

As an employer you should bend on this matter and ask if she will make and serve coffee if you are entertaining important clients in the office, and share the job the rest of the time, or make a deal . . . you will do something else if she will do this.

• DO NOT EVER ASK a secretary to take on the job of cleaning the office. Yes, you may ask her to organize your desk, you have the right to ask her to keep her own desk and area neat—but she should rightly assume that someone else will empty the wastebaskets and swab the deck. If you want your desk polished, either arrange it with the cleaning woman or do it yourself.

• PERSONAL TASKS such as banking are within the secretarial realm. You can ask her to go to the bank and make your deposits, get cash for you and stand on line. But she will do it on your time, not on her lunch hour. Errands for gifts for your spouse are strictly out of line. The implication here is if you can't spare the time to choose a personal gift for your own husband or wife, why are you married in the first place? If you're a workaholic, that's your problem. Keep your family off your secretary's back.

• SET FORTH your feelings about "visiting rights" in the office. Many secretaries like to have other secretaries visit regularly to discuss quasi-social matters. Or to have the hubby come by at lunchtime or after work every day and pick them up. If you don't want his body draped over her desk until she gets herself together, make it known from the start.

• BE REASONABLE about certain considerations. Remember that dentists and such also conduct nine-to-five hours. If your secretary is having root-canal work it may not be feasible to arrange it during nonworking hours. Don't be afraid to be human.

Questions like those above that may come up in the future should be covered at the interview. You must make the picture clear at the start. If there is a chance the secretary will not get a raise in six months, say so. Don't make any false promises, even if you think there's a good chance of such a raise. Unless you can put it in writing, don't promise it. If it happens in six months, you'll gain the gratitude then. If you have promised it and it doesn't materialize, you'll have one steamed secretary on your hands and you life will not go as smoothly.

If there is anything that you are not sure of, ask the applicant directly, "Do you object to this?" or what her feelings are on the matter. Don't leave anything to chance.

What You Want

When hiring a secretary, tell her what you expect of her as a professional.

Tell her you'll want her to work on the most important tasks first during the day, and as a general rule. And from that point on you should let her know what you consider to be the most important tasks.

Tell her that you expect her to be self-motivated. Past communicating certain urgent priorities, no boss should have to tell his secretary how to set up her day, or how to work—or even to ask her why she isn't working. If the work is not coming through as you expect it, then the secretary obviously has problems organizing her workday, and you should offer some advice—perhaps even sit down and arrange a schedule with her.

It really is difficult to know what to do as a boss at certain times. You may see your secretary reading the paper at her desk, and be unsure whether or not she is actually working. Other times you could swear every time you look at her she is typing the same letter, and hours have passed. The only way a boss can judge anything is by the results. If you are receiving the work in a reasonably efficient way and things are not delayed on a regular basis, you should not get bent out of shape about the fact that she doesn't "look busy."

Phone Work

Your secretary will be acting as your representative while she's on the job. You should set a pattern of how you want the phone answered at the office. It should be mentioned that at early levels an executive may think the casual approach is all right, but it's not. You should have your secretary answer the phone by saying, "This is Mr. [or Miss] Smith's line—Miss Johnson speaking." Using people's full names—Joe Smith or Jane Doe—is also acceptable. There is no reason for her to give the company name, and although a pleasantry such as "Good morning" is nice, it is much more businesslike to present information in a pleasant formal way.

A mumbled "Hello" or the single word "Yes?" is not an acceptable way to answer callers. Worse is the casually answered phone followed by an abrupt bounce into politeness when it turns out that the caller is "important." Is politeness to be reserved for the select few? It is as insulting to adopt a sudden polite manner for a VIP, who has already been slighted anyway, as it is to be careless about any caller.

Your rise upward is dependent on the overall image you present to the business world. Make sure you impart this to your secretary.

Should you ask your secretary to lie for you? If there is something you don't want someone to know, and your secretary is asked, give her an answer for him. She can say, "You'll have to discuss that directly with Mr. Jones. If you would like, I can pass on this question to him and he can get back to you." Do not ask your secretary to lie to your spouse. If you are having an affair on the side, don't tell your secretary. Just say that you are going to go to a meeting and that if your spouse calls she should say you'll meet him or her at such a time and place. Establish a precedent of not letting your secretary in on such matters, so that she won't ever have to lie for you. Don't involve your secretary in this kind of personal matter.

If you are a superbusy person it may be necessary to have your secretary place your calls. When this is the case, have her say she is calling for you and ask if it is convenient for the person to talk to you now, then put you on the call. The secretary should always alert you so that you won't keep the other person waiting too long on the line. Some people prefer to place their own calls. In either case, the secretary should know your preference before she starts the job.

If you deal with a lot of hotheads, arrogant execs or basically rude people, prepare your secretary for this so that she doesn't take it personally. And let her handle it from there.

DO: Back your secretary up as much as possible if she runs into a hassle on the phone. If the nature of your business requires her to deal with a lot of important nasties, then help her arrive at a way to steel herself against telling them what she really feels. In this case backing her up is giving her your private assurance that you appreciate what she must cope with.

DON'T allow your secretary to be anything less than you require on the phone. If you have an image you want presented to your public, you should insist on it.

After She Starts

Young executives, especially very young female executives, often feel confusion when playing boss to a secretary. Some treat a secretary as a lower-echelon nonperson and become callous and inhuman. Others, remembering their very recent tenure as assistants, try for a social relationship as well, and can soon become enmeshed in a twenty-four-hour nonfriendship.

A secretary is not a lower form of life; she is a professional who can help you get through your career. When you are not in the office, the secretary must know what you would do and convey your decisions to others. She must know what you really meant to say in that oddly worded letter to your biggest advertiser and either make it right or point it out to you.

To establish a real rapport with your secretary, you should have a series of meetings with her during the first week to make sure she has a full picture of who you are in the company, how you want things done, whom you deal with on a regular basis. If there are monsters in your professional life, tell her how you must deal with them, and have a question-and-answer session with her about such people. Let her know who your professional friends are, who requires special treatment from you, who may pose a threat to your career. Tell her whom to keep polite and silent with, who likes the more casual approach. The best way to bring these points home is to take them as they come, so that she won't get confused about whom you're talking about. But she should know at the start the names of the important honchos and honchas in your company.

Make no mistake: you must have these orientation meetings with your secretary. Otherwise you will leave the whole thing to succeed or fail on its own. It is always puzzling why young execs don't take the time to build this kind of rapport intentionally when the secretary is the one co-worker with whom anyone must have a close personal in-office relationship. We know of one young woman exec who went through so many secretaries in a year and a half that her company passed down a dictum that she had to keep the next secretary for a year, whether or not it worked out.

Don't Get Personal

As we said, a secretary may have an intimate knowledge of many professional and personal aspects of your life—necessarily. This does not mean you have to make her a part of your social and home life. Bosses and secretaries should meet in the morning and part in the evening and keep away from each other on weekends. If your mother or father is sick, get a friend or a nurse to care for them. Do not ask your secretary to check up on them in the hospital or at home. If you do, this will bind you to her with a special obligation, and you will not be able to command a certain discipline in the office. There is no reason why your spouse or lover should become social friends with your secretary. They may have a liking for each other when they meet in passing, but they should not be running off shopping together, deciding what color upholstery should go into your new car, or planning the holidays together. With the kind of changing corporate situations we have at present, these relationships can only lead to someone being taken advantage of, or of you being placed in compromising situations in the office.

If your son needs his term paper typed up, have him find someone else to do it, not your secretary. If your wife needs extra pâté from the gourmet shop, have the shop deliver it, not your secretary. If your wife has no time to get to Saks, have her wait until she has time, or have her call her sister.

You may have a very busy job which doesn't allow you much division between your free time and your office time. Your secretary may be expected to put in extra hours arranging your plane tickets, being there when you leave from the office, holding the fort while you're in Washington crumpling some senator's lapel. She still needs some time that belongs to her.

"I need my weekends," says one secretary. "I put in some

fifty hours a week, I get there early in the morning, leave late at night. If I'm not there my boss panics. So I make it clear that I don't answer the phone weekends. I may want to see a movie on TV, get my laundry done, or just *sit*. That's my time for me, and that's the bottom line."

DO: Establish a rapport with your secretary if you are in a career that requires you to make special demands beyond the call of duty. Some secretaries must take the approach that they are their jobs, more or less, rather than working at a job nine to five. If this is the devotion and stamina you require from the woman, make sure you are on the same wavelength.

DON'T make special demands unless the situation truly demands it. Your whole career may require such personal devotion and sacrifice from a secretary, or you may need these favors only periodically. Don't make your secretary's lot a thankless one.

The Pool

Secretaries who work in a pool are something akin to a "homeless" Renaissance painting and are often treated like Charles Dickens orphans. There usually is no specific boss; anyone who needs a letter typed or a report filed or something done fast can descend like an Asian warlord and raid the secretarial pool. Sounds a little dire, but that's about the way pool secretaries see themselves—and with good reason.

They generally are treated as machines; as possible sex partners by horny young execs; as robots who don't need to go to the water fountain, the rest room or the dentist. The good ones get the lion's share of the work, the cute ones get the lion's share of the passes. No one ever thanks them for anything. Everyone throws on them work that needs to be done ten minutes ago.

People are always interrupting them to try to get them to put aside someone else's work and do their work instead.

There is little camaraderie from their fellow secretaries. These pools can be ponds of gossip, innuendo and prying. There are constant petty envies, petty complaints, petty everything, since many of them are just typing away until they meet Mr. Right—or even Mr. Wrong.

As a person who must draw on these secretaries for clerical aid, you should develop a system to get the best possible work without alienating anyone else. Cultivate relationships with some of the secretaries in a pool and rely on them to do the things that need be done, instead of running out to demand and wheedle for things on the spur of the moment. But do not place the secretary in a compromising position so that she becomes an object of resentment or gossip to the other execs and secretaries.

It takes diplomacy at the start. Survey the pool and see how other execs treat the secretaries, and watch the reactions they get afterward. Decide which secretaries have done the most reasonable work for you, and begin a campaign of niceness. Ask them always if they are able to do something for you without coercion. Gravitate to the most amenable of your chosen few, and begin thanking them and telling them quietly that you like their work and appreciate it. By building up this subliminal goodwill you are developing people who will be more inclined to get to your work, since they will like you. Limit your compliments to the work; do not enter the realm of personal appearance or taste.

By choosing more than one secretary you will avoid flak from your peers. By choosing only one if you are a man and the secretary is a woman, you will incite gossip among the other secretaries, who may think the two of you are sleeping together. This is no idle consideration; experience proves it out. Secretaries in a pool are generally alert to any kind of spiciness that makes the workplace more intriguing. Many of them *want* to be objects of desire to executives. Whether you are a male or a female exec, play it safe on all levels and cultivate several secretaries.

It has been suggested that you rely on one person to make your travel arrangements, another for typing letters, another for something else.

Using secretaries from a pool is excellent training for dealing with a private secretary later on. It also may provide you with a private or shared secretary when you achieve a position where you don't have to use the pool anymore. You can take your favorite secretary from the pool with you, or make an offer if you go to another company. It's always an advantage to have a known quantity as your secretary when you're moving up.

DO: Exercise discretion when using the pool secretaries, especially if you are a man dealing with women. Do go to bat for a secretary who has served your needs well, when she has complaints or special needs of her own.

DON'T make promises. If you have the idea—or fantasy—of taking along a particular secretary when you move up, keep it to yourself until you can actually materialize the plan.

The Art of Giving

One area of quicksand between bosses and their secretaries is that of giving gifts. The best kind of gift to a secretary is always a bonus which comes via the company due to a boss's request. This is seldom possible unless you own the company or have enough corporate clout to demand a raise for your secretary every year. It's best for a boss to make a policy of limiting gifts to small items or cash items of a limited amount.

These days a limited amount could be as high as $100, if you make enough to warrant such a gift. Do not get into the habit of gifting your secretary on a regular basis. You can give a small item or a gift certificate on her birthday, limited to $25. Or take her to lunch and have flowers sent—which will no doubt take you over that $25 limit easily. There is nothing wrong with giving a secretary a bottle of champagne if you know she would get some fun out of it. Perfume is good; nylons are not. A sweater is acceptable, a pants suit is not. Cash in a card or a gift certificate is always appropriate.

Substantial gifts should come at Christmas and at no other time. Do not set a precedent for giving lavish gifts, because you will then expect yourself to keep it up year after year. If you take a business trip to Europe, you can bring back some item for her, since she has probably done superduty while you've been gone. If there are free trips available through the company's contacts, make them available to her when you can. If you receive a lot of gifts from business contacts at Yuletide, you can offer her a selection of some duplicate items.

It is best to make it a policy that she should not return your gifts in kind. You may find yourself in a gift exchange that she can't really afford. Make it clear that your gifts to her are to thank her for a job well done and are not meant to incite something in return. If she wants to give you some item once after a few years of happy working together, accept it graciously.

Thoughtfulness during what she knows is a busy time for you will really be appreciated: picking up some special pastry on the way to work; putting some flowers, or a single rose, on her desk periodically. If you are really well paid a nice gesture would be to have fresh flowers delivered to her desk every Monday, or a spray of some exotic flower. Depending on your position and salary level, these things fall into the area of small niceties. Certainly a middle-level exec could not afford such a gesture. But a big honcho making plenty of money or able to work it into his budget can make his secretary's day brighter in this manner.

The gifting should always be appropriate to the overall situation, and should be something not mentioned to other people in the office. Why set precedents that other secretaries will come to expect from their bosses? Part of having your own secretary is having a private kind of rapport on a professional basis. Just as no one should have a view of other private aspects of your life, so should your interaction with your secretary be kept private.

DO: Remember that day-to-day appreciation, consideration and gentility are much more important than a grand gesture during a holiday.

DON'T feel obliged to give gifts out of a sense of guilt. A once-a-year bonus is enough.

Spouses Go Home!

I once was attacked verbally on a TV show by a woman who thought I should have agreed that a wife should have final approval of her husband's secretary. I told the woman that she didn't have final approval of his yearly budget, the color of his office walls, or his co-workers, so she had no business interfering in this matter. Her husband was presumably hiring a secretary, not a concubine, I said. She hated that. I could have said more about marriage being based on trust, but that was her problem.

Wives and husbands need not pass judgment on the secretaries of their spouses. It is an insult to the secretary. It is as much as saying, "We think you might be a tramp, and we want to make sure you aren't." Unless your secretary is going to have the right to approve your wife's domestic handling of the kids, the budget and meals, your wife should keep her nose where it belongs. The same holds true if you are a married female executive. Your husband should never tell you who to hire or fire.

DO: Make your choice of a secretary based on business considerations.

DON'T hassle her with your marital problems, your marriage or your spouse's hangups.

CHAPTER 5

Basic Boss:

You Run the Show

"People who want to destroy things never take the wrong actions. . . . It is the ones who want to build who must watch the pitfalls."

Changing Focus

The moment arrives. The title is on the door, and the gray industrial carpeting is on the floor. You have been moved up. You are now at the first plateau of power. You are the boss. This is no time to panic. It is time to take stock of what lies before you—after a nice, cold bottle of champagne, of course—and make your plans for your new projects.

A thousand questions that you perhaps hadn't considered before arise suddenly. You realize how completely you are in charge of things. You have to hire and maybe fire people. You have to learn budgets and how they work. Budgets! Up to now all you had to do to get more money was whine to *your* boss. Now *you* are management.

Taking on such a position after being in what may be termed a creative position represents a subtle but significant break with the way you viewed your career before. Previously you were more insulated; you considered the company mostly in terms of what it could do for you. Now you have to adjust your thought processes and weigh what's good for the company against what's good for your employees while keeping a hook on what's good for you. Whereas earlier you had to please your boss and yourself —two people—now you must balance what the company wants against the need of your staff. You have new loyalties.

If you were a maverick before, you will have to soften and mature your attitudes. Your future is more dependent now on the goodwill of the people in upper management. And now you will have more direct interchanges with them without the blurring focus of your boss's intercessions. Before, your career was based primarily on producing; now it's based primarily on being diplomatic, political.

If you don't make a certain change in attitude and approach, you may find yourself experiencing something akin to frustration, even disillusionment. Suppose there were things that you handled directly, things that you perhaps loved to do, creative things. Suddenly you find they are taken out of your hands. The people who report to you handle these things now. You feel like a puppeteer. You have more free time—thanks a lot!—and you wonder what to do with it. The idle-hands syndrome strikes again. After being such a dynamo, and really honing your skills, suddenly you aren't supposed to do those things anymore.

In a sense you are back to square one, like when you were new on the job and green, and they didn't have enough yet to keep you busy until you knew more about the job. The thing you should be doing at this point is pretty much what you were doing then: learning the new job, only faster, and while you're training others into your old job.

The refocus here is not on your career goals, but on your new career attainments. You have to grow into a new you, so to speak. Instead of performing, you are influencing. You felt like a creative type before? Well, you still are. Now you must redefine your creativity within a wider framework. You are like an opera singer who has become a maestro or a diva. You can still do the stuff better than most people, only now you can tell others how to do it better as well. That's what being a boss means.

We all know what a boss is. We know we like the good ones and would like the bad ones to choke on their egg salad someday at lunch. We all know what we would do if we were king—or do we? Being a boss isn't as easy as it looks. Granted it can't possibly be as hard as some people make it, but there are a lot of things one has to learn once the medal has been struck and one's name is on the door. Learning to be a boss is like learning a whole new profession from the start. The way you first approach your new employees will make the difference as to whether or not you will be effective as a leader. The important thing here is not to let your triumph run away with you once you get promoted. One way to get a lead on this is to prepare yourself in Basic Boss. Decide what an effective manager and administrator does, and take if from there.

There are several basics that a boss must bear in mind if he or she wants to be successful at it. These concern the diplomatic area of bossing, and they are essential to doing the job.

• ACCEPTANCE AND REJECTION. Earlier we mentioned that the need for acceptance is a powerful factor in the human psychology. The fear of rejection, and the humiliation and embarrassment that accompany such an event, are also extremely strong motivators. When people experience rejection, for example in the form of a reprimand from the boss, they go through agonies of embarrassment and even shame. Some people can cope with it, others have a real dread of it. When you compliment someone who works for you, you are in essence saying yes to him. This is acceptance. It is a powerful tool in building loyalties and in motivating people to work well and to put forth their best efforts on the job. This is a positive motivator.

When you snarl at someone who works for you, when you fail to comment favorably or you comment negatively on an employee's work, you are saying no to him. You are rejecting his work, and by projection rejecting him. You are playing on an employee's fear of rejection. This is not an effective tool, because it places a confusing factor, that of fear, on the person. Under such psychological pressure he may not be able to perform as intelligently as the person who has a positive motivation. The person also may hate you and find ways to undermine your position. This will place an added burden on you, and the cycle continues on and on.

• PRAISING. This is a form of acceptance—an excellent tool and one which is as mother's milk to an employee. Even if a person knows he is doing a good job, he needs to hear that said by the boss. Do not deprive your people of words of praise. These are like little reinforcements of their validity as people in the company. You can even tell a person his work is not up to par if you couch it in positive terms. You can compliment the person on his good points as a way of contrasting areas where he is weak. A positive way of telling someone he is screwing up is to provide positive suggestions and advice on how to do the job better. So you can use the tool of praising as a way both to praise and to "reprimand." Either way you will get the results you want: better employees.

• SECURITY. People worry constantly about being fired. It's like herpes: when it hasn't happened to you, it looms like a dark shadow over your consciousness. A boss can take the high road and use the tools of acceptance to remove this pressure from his people as much as possible; or he can take the low road and constantly use the threat of termination to whip them into line. It has been shown that people respond better to the high road, since such a tactic removes unnecessary pressures from the workplace and they can concentrate on doing the jobs that they enjoy. If you make people want to come to work you will have fewer problems with resentments, fewer demands for raises all the time, and fewer complaints about conditions.

• MOTIVATING. A boss should consider employee motivation as one of his biggest tasks. Your people should want to work. Part of your job is creating an environment, as much as possible, that your people will like, one they will look forward to coming to every day, and one in which they are happy to work. This is done in part by taking steps to make sure people have as pleasant a physical space as possible, and by creating a psychological ambiance as well. This can be even more important. The boss must project an air of caring about what his people are feeling toward their work and workplace. This is done through keeping yourself visible; by accepting problems as solvable; by instilling a sense of being in charge—which is done by handling the problems that come your way; by making decisions based on competence. If your people trust you, they will feel more comfortable, and more motivated, to put out their best work.

• RESPECT. People must respect you, must believe that you are the right person to be the boss. It is not important that they respect you as an upstanding citizen, or as an admirable parent to your children, but as a boss. It is not even important that they like you, as long as they feel you are handling the area that affects their careers in a way they believe in. As long as people feel you have access to the solutions to office problems, as long as they believe you will be fair in your attitudes about their needs for money and benefits, as long as they feel you respect them, not view them as so many androids, dispensable and replaceable, people will respect you as boss.

Respect is engendered through making intelligent decisions, not flighty ones. People respect a boss who is predictable in his responses—one they can depend on to do certain things. You may have quirks, but if they are predictable personality traits, and not sudden flare-ups of irrational behavior like shooting stars, they are acceptable and can be respected.

In essence, people will always respect a boss, even a mediocre one, who they feel has the intelligence and experience and human intuition to make the right decisions. Your people must believe that you are capable of doing your job, since how you do it affects how they do theirs.

DO: Try to remain open to your employees' needs as humans as well as workers. Find ways to express the attitude that you want them, not some other people, to do their jobs.

DON'T be afraid to verbalize what to you may seem to be inane compliments about their work. Genuine praising is never inane. It always works well for the giver and the receiver. Don't minimize the importance of praising as a tool for getting maximum efficiency from people.

Am I Truly Qualified to Lead?

In business, as in politics, seldom does the candidate ever stop to ask the key question: Am I truly qualified to lead? Getting the prize is the only consideration. Winning is all, and it isn't until you're sworn in and installed in your own version of the Oval Office that it hits you: What on earth am I doing here? It is true that there is nothing quite like on-the-job training for producing really fine execs, but you should have had some forethought and looked into the nuts and bolts of being boss before you got there.

In large bureaucratic types of companies, such as Con Edison in New York, telephone companies and such, there are formal training programs provided all along the line of moving up. Seminars are available, as are reference books and manuals, instructions on how to handle this and that problem. Personnel problems have solutions set down on paper, and all through the companies there are operation policies that everyone basically knows about and can turn to. Although these don't necessarily make life simple, they do provide some nice fibrous rules that a new supervisor or manager can bounce off of in moments of panic.

When you do not have such a bible to turn to, you must develop a sense of what makes people tick. The basis of that we discussed above. You must also develop a technique to arrive at solutions to problems when you are puzzled about what to do. If the problem involves a direct work problem, you can turn to your knowledge of the business and make a decision based on your background and experience. "People" problems are something else again, and these are the ones that send new bosses out on long lunch hours.

A boss of mine used to use the technique of letting the people solve the problem for him. He would sit down and discuss any problem that came up, on the spot, and let the people involved talk it out until they provided a solution. Then he would seize on the one that looked most acceptable and "decide" on that. By his letting the people blow off steam, they felt better, and because they got a decision from him they were happy. This is a good technique for anyone who doesn't automatically see the solution to a problem clearly, or who is not secure enough to trust his or her own judgment at a certain time.

Remember that each problem is pregnant with its own solution. The boss must develop some midwife's technique to bring it forth. A good boss listens, probably more than he talks. Remember that the people who work for you are the best sources of solutions to problems. Let them talk, since sometimes that is the only way they will flash on the solution. Your forte as a boss is to be able to recognize the solution and "decide" on it. This is a perfectly valid way to function as a boss. You don't have to have the answers—just have the ability to find them.

Much of what passes for management these days is in reality nothing more than guesswork. Sometimes it works, sometimes it doesn't. As long as you can maintain a strong communications atmosphere in your office, as long as your people are free to talk, you should have no problem finding answers.

A very real problem today with bosses is that very few people want to take on the responsibility of supervising. People want power, people want prestige, but the actual work of leading makes people—some people—so insecure that they want to hide out in their offices. Many people think being boss means bossing people around. In truth being boss means being a constant diplomat, a decision-maker and an arbitrator. All the old clichés come true now. He who would lead must serve. Do unto others as you'd have them do unto you. You catch more flies with honey than with vinegar. As we who are about to die salute you.

DO: Give talking-things-out a chance, even if it takes a little longer. Wrong decisions take more time to reverse.

DON'T abdicate on decision making. Don't panic if you don't have an immediate solution. Don't be rushed. Remember that a mediocre decision is better than no decision at all.

What Makes a Good Boss?

Most people probably would agree on how they want the boss to act: benevolent, nice, understanding, helpful, generous—that sort of thing. Moving into the real world, there are some important qualities that do make a good boss—not necessarily a boss who is good *to* people, although that couldn't hurt, but someone who is good to work for while producing for the company's good as well.

Delegating Authority

This is one of the essential duties of a good boss: the ability to give assignments, then let the person do his or her work with confidence. A common problem among neophyte or even experienced bosses is that they do not know how to let go. They want to do it all themselves, and never trust anyone else to be able to do it "their way."

My favorite lousy boss had this flaw. Unable to give directions on how she wanted things done, she would hand an assignment to a newly hired person, say, "Do this," and stalk back to her office. The new person would wonder exactly what "Do this" meant in relation to that particular piece of business, and would sit in stark fear while his stomach turned to ice water. Of course the work could not ever be right under these circumstances; even the Foreign Legion provides a few basic instructions before sending their boys into the fray. So the woman who was boss could never get any kind of acceptable work—since only she carried the mystery of what acceptable work was in her eyes, and every new employee was off to a bumpy start. I never knew anyone who worked for this woman for longer than sixteen months. She was eventually shoved out herself and at last report carried the secret of "acceptable work" to her grave.

> **DO:** Trust your own judgment to oversee production so that you can feel secure about delegating authority.
>
> **DON'T** start laying your fears on the people you've delegated authority to.

Communicating

What does delegating responsibility mean? First, the boss must discuss how he or she wants the work performed. The time frame required for completing the work must be communicated.

The boss must also be available for answering questions during the completion of the job. This isn't a College Board test, this is trying to get the work done right. Everyone runs into snags, and it's better for your people to come to you rather than try to second-guess you because you get so upset when anyone asks you a simple question. A good boss does not make a fuss and call people stupid just because a question arises. A good boss also does not try to give the impression that he or she is so damn weary because no one else seems able to do anything and he or she has to watch everyone every minute.

A good boss should ask about the assignment after a certain reasonable length of time to find out how the work is going, whether there are problems, whether the deadline will be met, or whether the whole thing is collapsing and everyone is afraid to tell him. This checking up should be done in a routine way, not with a sort of inner tension that makes people think the boss is worried that it won't happen.

Part of this delegating of responsibility includes the appropriate response whenever such assignments are delayed. It never does any good to start screaming for things at deadline time. If you had kept yourself posted on progress the missed deadline could perhaps have been avoided. Staff people have a responsibility to tell you if it looks as though something will be running into a snag. You should make it clear that you understand that circumstances, not just incompetence or stupidity, cause such problems. By inquiring into the reasons for problems, you can establish a sense of confidence and cooperation among your people so that you will have a better chance of avoiding potentially problematic situations. If the screw-up was not caused by anyone's temporary insanity, then look toward a solution; don't start yelling and trying to pin blame somewhere. It is never the end of the world if something fails to come through on time—unless you run the switchboard on the nuclear hotline.

It is a fact that people who work under conditions that free them from the screaming scourge of impeachment and blame will make fewer mistakes. People who have been maligned by a boss's tongue on a regular basis tend to miss deadlines, or produce second-rate work. Be sure they don't get blamed. These behavior patterns breed a most unproductive work environment.

> **DO:** Ask for progress reports on projects that you need to stay on top of. No sense losing control when things are crucial. This is a legitimate way to keep tabs on people without riding them.

> **DON'T** make yourself incommunicado waiting for disaster so that you can swoop down and lambast everyone in sight. Don't be unavailable.

Giving Directions

Some people never learn how to tell someone how to do something that they have been doing for years. The basic point to remember here is that the way to tell someone how to do something is to tell him how *you* do it. One of the best bosses I ever knew did just that with new staff people. He didn't sit down and give a "Watch me" seminar, but as each new thing came up, when it appeared that the employee didn't have a hook on how to do a particular job, he would say, "What I always do is this . . . ," then clearly and pleasantly reveal his own work methods that worked for him. He didn't require anyone to photocopy his patterns or go to Coleco and have them softwared in. If the methods worked for his employee, fine. If it just provided a pattern to vary from, that was fine, too. He taught his people much that was valuable in later years.

DO: Accept a person's methods as valid if they prove effective, even though they may differ from your own.

DON'T try to force your methods on someone. Suggest them, use them as examples, then leave to the employee the decision as to whether or not to accept your ways.

The Big Picture

A good boss maintains a sense of the outside world. Don't worry so much about formalities such as nine-to-five punctuality when your staff is producing and achieving things that are admirable. Remember that your people are not only working for you but are also working for themselves. Accept the fact that some of them are using this as a steppingstone to another job—perhaps yours or one like yours elsewhere. Accept the fact that your own position there is ultimately a temporary one. You may want to move on, and you should develop an atmosphere that will enable you to do so.

Too many bosses achieve their first big job and clutch. They get scared. They are afraid of losing it. They start looking inward for ways to protect what they have rather than looking to where they can go. As soon as a boss starts hanging on for dear life, his effectiveness goes to hell. He is no longer working for the company, he is trying to survive at all costs. He will sacrifice anyone who seems to threaten that survival, and the company will lose out on quality personnel and products as a result. Always remember that if you were able to move up at all, you can move up again and stay valuable if you continue producing what is wanted.

DO: Enjoy being a boss at a specific time and place.

DON'T start sacrificing your people on the altar of your insecurities.

Ways to Praise

I was told of one boss who admitted to a longtime executive woman that he was just unable to give people compliments. He would merely shrug his shoulders when she came in excited to tell him about some new client she had roped after months of selling and convincing. He was noncommittal about everything. "In twenty years, my boss has never praised me with one word," the woman said. "I helped build his business, I'm responsible for millions of dollars to his company. If I didn't get so much gratification from other aspects of my job I'd always have a bad taste in my mouth. When I get that reaction from him it suddenly becomes *his* company. When I don't think of him I feel I'm achieving something valuable and doing something creative for a company that is a part of me. It's a real problem."

A boss should make sure that his people are credited for their achievements by someone besides himself. Some companies provide a tool by which to do it in the form of written reports issued twice a year evaluating everyone's performance. Then the credit becomes part of the company record. It becomes more difficult to have your talents recorded in less bureaucratic companies which prefer to let aggressiveness and competition carry the day; talented people are pushed to the wings while people whose main talent is aggressiveness move into positions they are not always suited for.

DO: Make the effort and the occasions to vocalize credit.

DON'T hesitate to write a private memo to someone who has done a good job. A written memo saying you like the way a certain project was handled, or congratulating him or her on some coup, can have an even happier effect than a spoken word. Do it!

Financial Support

A boss should support his employees' legitimate requests for financial compensation. A person should not have to fight both his boss and the company for a raise. Part of a boss's job is determining when an employee deserves a raise—and handling the situation with support in other ways, even psychologically, when a raise is not able to be granted.

Too many companies are cheap as a matter of policy, and this places an unnecessary burden on their employees. As a boss you should put forth an honest effort to help deserving employees obtain their raises.

It is always difficult for a supervisor who must sit between company policy and employees' needs for raises. You cannot be a revolutionary firebrand and ruin your reputation with management, and you cannot alienate your staff by taking a hard line. One way to maintain relations with both sides is to present a fair and urgent appeal when there is a real need to get more money for a member or members of your staff—even if it means you come up with a plan to find the money. And you should keep the staff member informed of what your efforts entail, always cautioning him that you may not have enough of a case to offset company policy. In smaller companies the financial crunch may be real enough that the employee will have to understand that whatever his own need the money is not there to give. Few larger companies are unable to find some money somewhere to provide raises for individuals. When the head of a small company wastes money on expensive lunches, gifts or trips that are not necessary, his employees will not believe there is no money available for them.

As an executive, remember that you do have a responsibility to the people who work for the company and they have a right to expect fair treatment when they must make sacrifices for the good of the company.

DO: Be honest with your people when raises are not forthcoming. Be honest about your efforts or nonefforts to back them up. If you can't ask for a raise at a particular time, be straightforward about it.

DON'T go after raises for dubious employees. If someone is not working up to par, don't pretend that you are backing them up in a request for a raise. Provide honest suggestions for improvement so that they can be aware of shortcomings. Don't ever give anyone a raise unless you are absolutely sure he or she will be retained in your employ on a permanent basis. It will reflect badly on you if you request raises and then capriciously fire someone who never was going to work out in the first place.

We Don't Have a Barrel of Money

When you work for a company that is not able to—or just won't—pay competitive salaries, you as a boss must go to greater lengths to keep your people happy. You must provide a great place to work so that they'll think hard about leaving for better money. No matter what the salaries, you still have to get employees to work if the office is to function. Even nonprofit organizations, charity foundations, maintain organizational systems of authority and cooperation to operate properly. The lines of authority must be kept clearly defined.

An executive in a nonprofit company suggests accommodations in these areas:

• JOB SECURITY. By choosing carefully whom you hire, you can refrain from firing people.

• PRESTIGE. Because of the respect and admiration his prestigious organization receives, the people who work there have more social clout. They're proud of where they work.

• FREEDOM. In dress, time spent in the office, approach to job. Although a certain amount of style is required, there are no hard-and-fast rules about coats and ties. People are not locked into the nine-to-five workday. Since there are few deadline pressures, and no need to produce for profit, people can work at their own pace in a relaxed manner.

• FREEBIES. To shows, exhibits, openings that would cost money, or more money, if attended without the backup of the organization.

• CARING. Here the boss is not so aloof, can adopt a more demonstrative approach when listening to personal ideas. Also, there can be more out-of-office socializing than in a more commercial company.

• LACK OF STRESS. Without the profit motive, here the pressure is already limited. If there is a profit involved, the boss should take steps to reduce pressures wherever possible.

DO: Maintain your prerogatives as a boss. Expect and let it be known that you expect full and competent performance on the job. The mere fact that the money is low is no reason to accept part-time work. Remember that your employees agreed to work for that money, so sloughing off is not acceptable.

DON'T allow yourself to be used. As long as you are offering an opportunity to learn, to work at a satisfying job, and are making efforts to offset the lack of money, you are providing many things perhaps not available at other jobs.

Handling Screw-ups

One basic fact that you as boss must keep in mind is that when you delegate responsibility you are responsible for what happens. Your employee is responsible for doing a job, but you are responsible for the employee. This is why it's so important to have people whom you can trust working for you.

A mature person as boss can handle periodic snarls without going off the deep end. Remember that there are always ups and downs. Don't hold an employee up to blame just to save your own skin. If someone does make mistakes you have the avenues open to you to reprimand, to discuss the problem or, if it goes on too long, to fire the person.

When pointing out mistakes, remain cool. Don't rant and scream. It only clouds up the issue and makes the screaming the point, not correcting the mistake. Give the person a chance to explain—even to save face. Accept certain mistakes as inevitable, and see if you can't both come up with a way to correct the problem. At times the solution is to accept the loss incurred and try not to let it happen again. There are many situations in business where you can correct and recover. If you can, do it, and let happiness be the order of the day. If you can't, let the person learn from the mistake.

Take this same approach if the mistake affects you and was made outside your own department. Don't ever try to make a joke out of someone's errors as a way of accepting them. The best approach is always to minimize the discussion about the mistake itself and approach errors with solutions. A mistake is not necessarily an indication of incompetence. Mistakes are a daily part of business and should be accepted as part of anyone's job.

Delegating blame is not the same as scapegoating; it is another form of delegating responsibility. If, for example, you are not the kind of boss who can come up with solutions to problems, there is nothing wrong with making the person who is most capable of finding a solution to a problem come up with one. If someone has made a mistake, there is nothing wrong with telling him to come up with a way to correct it. This is a very legitimate part of the overall parcel of delegating responsibility. You as the boss make the decision about how to define responsibility.

> **DO:** Ask for a professional solution, and offer advice if you have any.
>
> **DON'T** get hung up on "punishing" someone just because he screwed up.

Meetings, Meetings

Meetings are the best way for a boss to gather ideas from the people best able to advise him. Your staff is most closely informed about the normal activities of your department. These people have the best viewpoint of what your needs are and in which direction you must head to improve production. They know the mistakes being made, the pitfalls of the past, the client's mind. Regular staff meetings on a regular—even daily—basis are highly recommended, even though many members of the staff will see it as an intrusion into their own schedules. Make sure your people see the value of these meetings. For one thing, there is a tendency in an office for people to grow extremely insular. When this happens you have a bunch of mini-bosses each of whom thinks he or she is absolutely right about the way things should be done. A frequent exchange of ideas helps them view one another's talents and develop respect—or not—for one another's viewpoints. In any event, it maintains your position as the final authority and lets the staff view one another's thinking processes.

Some bosses insist that during the meeting each member of the staff come up with a specific number of new ideas—when ideas are required as a normal part of the type of business—or new ways to improve production or working conditions or whatever.

Besides gleaning suggestions directly from the people most involved, it enables people to complain in the form of positive suggestions for change, and to voice them in front of everyone. This gives the person a chance to get an immediate reaction about his ideas from other people he works with, and provokes interchange. It may be that a person will find that his complaint is his own personality quirk and that no one else minds something. Or maybe he has hit a common nerve. It further helps communication because some people will discuss ideas with other co-workers before the meetings and you will find more participation, more productivity and an increase in excellence among your staff.

DO: Allow the contributor of an accepted idea to head up the project.

DON'T ridicule ideas which are not acceptable.

Pro Tem

Many bosses do not like to have meetings because they don't know how to handle them. The technique is simple in the extreme. Write down your own ideas; write down the positive achievements of your staff in the past week or weeks; talk about lagging points after that, then ask for reactions from the staff. After that, ask each person to present his or her ideas. Write them down, with a notation of who the donors were so that you can refer to them with a credit line in the future. Or ask for memos. It is extremely important not to credit the wrong person, nor to make the idea something that came out of the staff as a whole in these meetings; everyone will remember whom the idea belonged to, and you will come across as unfair.

It is a good idea to include lower echelons in some meetings when feasible. This institutes a feeling of being part of the staff in a real way, lets people know what it is they are fighting for at such lousy salaries and makes people want to make things work better. Cooperation in meetings always improves the final product as well as the day-to-day working atmosphere.

Coffee and goodies are also a good idea at these meetings. We had a boss who always made the effort to have a different special kuchen or pastry delivered to ooh and ah over. It was a sort of little thank-you gift and made people look forward to the meetings. He also would insist that the service people leave the coffee urn on all day on these occasions so that the meetings took on a special importance.

DO: Emphasize the importance of the meetings by the times you schedule them. Perhaps 10 A.M. on Mondays to kick off the week. Or the more barbaric 3:30 P.M. Friday afternoons to point up the fact that the work week doesn't end on Thursday?

DON'T allow a casual attitude to infiltrate. If the meeting starts at a certain hour, expect people to be ready at that hour. Too often the starting time sludges into a long haul as people laze in, take coffee, schmooze and scratch and yawn. Let your own attitude and demeanor set the tone.

Good and Bad Intentions

The good boss does not moralize or try to justify his actions. There should be no reason to do so. If you act with the right intention, you will not have to agonize later. The biggest crippler in any difficult business situation is guilt. If you have come to a hard decision, say to fire someone, and it is the correct action to take, there is no reason to allow guilt to invade the issue. It only places you in a vulnerable position and you may make concessions you'll regret later on. It can appear that you perhaps have not taken the correct action, or are not sure enough of your decisions to back them up. Guilt, fear, wanting to be liked are all weaknesses when they fuzz your rational decisions.

Many people cannot cope with the emotional pressure of taking actions such as firing, reprimanding, acting out of economic necessity, refusing raises. All of these things should be approached with the correct intent, that of maintaining the function and efficiency of your department. These should not be emotional decisions.

If you do act out of ulterior motives, then of course you can go ahead and feel guilty. Using people as scapegoats to cover your own lack of ability is one area where you deserve to suffer pangs of remorse. If you are protecting yourself against a backstabbing co-worker or underling, that is another matter. No one should feel bad about staying alive when under direct attack.

People who do indulge in actions that don't arise out of legitimate career needs usually find themselves enmired both in feelings of guilt and in the trap of committing human sacrifice to stay in business. There is no such thing as propitiating the gods with one human sacrifice, not in business any more than in *King Kong*. Once you've decided to blame someone else for things not working, you're committed to keep coming up with more and more scapegoats or admitting that you are, and always were, the blameworthy one. After a while, of course, your admission won't be necessary. You'll probably be legendary for your little murders and someone will decide you're fair game, too.

DO: Go with your rational decisions. Remember that your intentions must govern your inner reactions.

DON'T go so far in expiating your guilt in advance that you put up with an incompetent for months on end after making the decision to terminate.

Boss's Etiquette

As a boss you are under a greater stricture to mind your manners, since there is no one but yourself to tell you when you are out of line—unless you have a really sharp secretary. It is true that a boss *can* usually behave any way he wants in an office situation; but you should not take that attitude. It only leads to a loss of efficiency and cuts down on the respect and coöperation you'll get from other people.

There is no place for anger in an office setting, yet some bosses use it as a regular tool. You should never berate someone who works for you, and especially not in front of his peers. This mistake is made by construction foremen and company presidents alike. It never looks good and it always breeds hatred. As a boss your greatest tool is your people's desire to work for you, to make you look good, and they will do this only if their self-esteem is high. Constant bad temper, insults, talking down, scornful remarks—none of these will serve you well as a boss.

DO: Make amends privately to a recipient of your anger, even when your blowup was based on an upsetting event. By admitting that your response was not appropriate you will show that you are able to check your own behavior and will engender a deeper feeling of trust and respect.

DON'T overreact to the overreaction. Apologize quietly, and in private, and drop it from your mind. The reason for keeping the apology private is to avoid a distasteful look-at-how-magnanimous-I-am display. Don't doubt that your apology will be noted without your help.

Overtalking

"The thing wrong with my boss is he doesn't leave anything unsaid, so you never know what has priority and what can wait. Everything comes at you at the same level. He talks about having a copy made with the same urgency as contacting an expert for research information."

A good boss is selective about what he talks about and how he talks about it. Some bosses will carry on about someone coming in five minutes late and carry on in the same way if someone forgot to include shipping costs in a budget. As a result no one hears what he has to say about anything, since everything is going to spark a high dudgeon, and everything becomes irrelevant.

Ego Trips

I was told once of a self-reverent executive who had gained some fame in his own field of endeavor. He decided somewhere along the line that he should go on to become a Living Legend. Each morning he held a "Me Meeting," whereat he would regale his staff with his triumphs with this or that person the night before. Although it was boring, his staff began to slough off on the work and spend most of their time, to put it delicately, sucking up to the LL. His ego became so ridiculously inflated the company had to fire him; he had become an embarrassment, and his effectiveness had been undermined.

DO: Look at what you are doing. Remember that the sun rises every morning whether or not you have a title on the door.

DON'T accept compliments, gifts or flattery from the people who work for you. Don't make nourishing your ego a condition of keeping a job.

Expressing New Leadership

There are several ways to approach a staff of people as their new boss. The one thing that must be done is to assert the fact that you are the boss. It does not have to be stated like Little Caesar taking over the South Side. Present yourself as a new person welcoming the people who are already there. You can state such things as "We will probably make some changes about such and such,'' respond to suggestions with statements like ''I'll consider that when making the decisions'' or ''. . . when we make the final decision.''

It's always a psychological help to use the editorial ''we'' in certain conversations to emphasize that you are the ''we'' in question. This small word goes far toward locking in your image as the new leader, without squashing anyone's ego.

If you plan to be an aloof boss, you can set a cordial formal friendliness at the start. It never goes across well to be too cold and unapproachable at the beginning. It will work against you ultimately, because you will never have an insight into the way people think. You should always try to make sure you involve all of your staff in the projects, ask for their thinking, and get as many heads into the work as you have available.

I had a friend who was extremely good at his job but had problems staying in any given company. Each time, he would be terminated because of some personality conflict. When he landed another job he told me he had just made friends with the receptionists, the mail-room people and the petty-cash lady. I asked him if he also planned this time to lavish some of his debonair charm on the people who could do him some good—his boss, the officers of the company, the ones who could make and break him. This question seemed to strike home.

It is all well and good to be friends with the lower echelons of the company, but if you are an executive you must first identify with and relate to your peers. It is nice to have the mail-room people on your side, but they have to deliver your mail whether you expend a lot of energy on them or not—and they probably don't care that much if you jaw with them about the Super Bowl.

It is essential to have your priorities straight. You are in business to make a career, make money, make a name for yourself. You need not make fast friends with people you probably have little in common with.

DO: Retain a certain respect for your position, while staying human.

DON'T waste time expending your vital energies where it won't do you or anyone much good.

DO: Remember that you represent your title as well as yourself. Do not be afraid to use the clout of that title to demand a certain respect. Remember, the authority is invested in the title, and you have the right to exercise that authority.

DON'T forget that the expression of leadership is literally the expression of it—in words. Speak as a leader, not as a wheedler.

Your Rights as the New Boss

In some companies the new boss coming in to take charge of a department has a right to restructure it as he or she sees fit. In other companies this is more of a privilege, and employees' rights are held to be prime considerations. It always helps when you have the freedom to cast off the people you can't work with, or people who have managed to hold on to jobs that they aren't qualified to do.

These days, due to capricious managers, special legislation and certain corporate policies, it is important that you detail in writing exactly why you want to fire each person. If it is an intangible, you should make it clear that you have specific needs in mind for the future and require someone of quite different qualifications. It is important not to appear to be capricious in firing people who have put in some time in a company. They may be old favorites, and even though you are supported in your choice while doing it, it is important to back up your changes with solid reasons. Then if something goes amiss in the future, your reputation won't fly to pieces with the people who hired you.

Remember that whatever the company policy where you work, all ruling members of any company want to appear to be benevolent and fair to their employees—even if it is not true. It is important not to tarnish this image, fictional as it may be. In some companies the image is all they have. And one thing that any up-and-coming young exec must remember is not to make them "up there" look bad.

Taking Stances

Being a boss involves taking stances. You must act and react to situations while maintaining a professional distance. Yet you must also remain human. Some stances are used on the spot. Others are permanent stances, involved in setting your style as a leader. For example, if there is a pressing deadline that must be met, you may adopt an "urgency stance" to bring home the importance of the deadline to your staff. You may speak in a restrained way as if holding back the urgency whenever discussing the matters pertaining to the deadline. You may send out signals that you are always on your way somewhere but are stopping to give some fast minutes to this or that person.

During this time you may hear yourself stressing polite words in an almost testy way. You can be forgiven if you seem distracted, since everything must take second place to the deadline. A hurried conversation may start like this:

"Excuse me, Mr. Jones, I wanted to ask you about these mechanicals."

You would say something like "*Yes,* Harry!," stressing the "yes," as if it were important to remind yourself not to be impatient with Harry for stopping you, and to show Harry how much energy you are expending to be polite. The stance is that Harry had better have a good reason for asking you something.

Some people adopt other kinds of stances, such as the Stance of Dismay, something like the reaction of a *grande dame* who is addressed directly by the plumber about her leak. This is used to express classy ire about something that one of your staff members has done that you disapprove of. I had a boss who always would say, "I am dismayed that you haven't got to this matter yet," and furrow her brow worriedly.

The Stance of Financial Ruin is a good one as well. It's the stance of a dire emergency that threatens the company's very existence. Seldom is it a real emergency, but it helps the company demand more effort from the employees while refusing to pay any more money until the emergency has passed. Although it's true that many companies do face financial ruin, many bosses also will hype up a minor setback to take advantage of the moment, scare employees into making sacrifices that are in no way relative to the real situation.

The Stance of Aloofness is necessary, though difficult for many to use. Remember that it can be detrimental to be a boss and a friend to a person at the same time. It's advisable to keep the friendliness as part of the weave of office life and avoid socializing with employees. There is a certain amount of posing that is necessary to maintain your authority as boss. Certain attitudes are expected from those in higher positions. People in lower positions enjoy such stances, since it gives them something to aim for, admire or read about in the *National Enquirer*. Gossip about higher-ups is fun.

It is part of the human condition to play roles, adopt mannerisms, play at being one person in one situation and adopt the trappings of another aspect of your personality in another. Societies where such elite fun-raising is proscribed are pretty deadly places. A visit to East Berlin will illustrate that.

The way to maintain your stance is by establishing patterns where professionalism, not coziness, is the rule. When someone makes an inroad toward getting to know you better, you simply abstain from making follow-up comments, and instead make a comment that will point the conversation toward areas relating to work.

> Example:
>
> "Boss, I saw you going into the movies last night. How did you like the movie?"
>
> "It wasn't bad. I want to ask you about the Buford account—when can we present them with our proposal?"

By maintaining distance in general office relationships you can keep certain areas of your personality a mystery.

> **DO:** Avoid stupid or snobbish stances for no reason. Do act out the part of executive when you have such a position. Incorporate it as part of your own personality and style, but retain the

impression that you have achieved something valid and are discreetly aware of it.

DON'T make yourself ridiculous by constantly referring to how great you are. Balance your act.

I Want Them to Like Me

Is it necessary for you as a boss to be liked by your staff? Important, perhaps, but not necessary. Being liked is not a key to functioning well in the job. It's much more important to engender a sense of respect for yourself as a competent professional. If you do, your people will be more inclined to try to please you, while taking on responsibility for those parts of the job that they legitimately should not pass on to you.

"Because my staff senses that I want them to like me, they see me as a soft touch," one department manager said. "So they run to me with every little problem, every argument, every difference of opinion they may have with merchants, suppliers or people in the department. So every time someone doesn't get something he or she wants, I have to listen to how the vice-president of cosmetics 'wants a reshoot of a layout and there's nothing wrong with it.'

"Eventually you have to tell them to solve certain problems themselves. Otherwise you become like a single parent with three kids who are always pulling on you for every little crayon or TV show."

Utilize your right to refuse to be involved. The same tactic can be used when you have staffers who constantly bring in problems for you to solve while they stare blankly out the window smoking or chewing gum. If someone is in the habit of dumping on you, involve the person in the search for the solution.

Example:

"Boss, this mechanical is wrong and I thought you'd want to see it. I can't seem to get Production to listen to me." (Smoke; chew; stare.)

"Tell me where it's wrong, and what you feel should be done to correct it."

"Well, there's this, and this."

"Fine. Now take it to Production and have them do this and this."

"Should I tell them you said to?"

"I don't think there should be a problem getting the corrections made—they're fairly standard practice."

DO: Support your staff people in matters where they are right and in matters relating to their work.

DON'T take part in emotional squabbles, or let yourself become a wailing wall for every nit that wants to be picked.

DON'T be afraid of a potential fight or flare-up. Create an atmosphere where infighting is not the proper response to situations in your department. Adopt a rational approach to complaints, and insist on people cooling down and presenting valid complaints—and only valid complaints—in a calm, professional, step-by-step manner.

Gauging Problems

Whenever there is something wrong in your office, you as a boss must find out whether the system is at fault or the people. If you find there is a backlog of work, you should gauge whether or not you need more people, or if the people you have aren't able to handle the work for some reason. A boss must always check out the validity of the system in use in his office before making forays against the efficiency of his people.

Ask for suggestions. Never forget that the people doing a job are best qualified to tell you where the inefficiencies are. Everyone has his own complaints about how things are set up. If certain systems do not facilitate work efficiency, don't take the position that the system is sacred and the people dispensable. People have certain needs at work. You as the boss are in a position to help them obtain these needs and to improve your company's situation. Don't divorce your staff's needs from the needs of the company. By maintaining a dynamic attitude toward systems and methods you can continually improve overall efficiency and morale.

DO: Involve your staff in problem-solving sessions whenever possible. Keep an open ear for complaints, since they reflect the true moods and unspoken resentments harbored by your people. Use complaints as bellwethers of morale. If your staff people complain a lot, start trying to get at the roots of the real problems by having open discussions and drawing them out.

DON'T take the stance that you shouldn't try to solve some important problems that don't seem to be your province. Sometimes a boss must extend his boundaries when morale is affected strongly. If there are resentments about co-workers smoking, hygiene, loudness or bickering, and efficiency is affected, take steps to change the situation, or help to change it.

Your Actions/Their Reactions

In any situation where the boss has a capricious ego the people who work under him have to find ways to deal with his unpredictable actions. The boss should be asking himself if he is acting in the best interests of the company, but if he doesn't—or if his answer is always yes—then the people under him must accommodate. Business then becomes an exercise in political behavior.

Some lower-level executives handle these situations very well by "talking out" problems until the capricious boss is brought around to the right decision. This is time-consuming, but it is a way to get things straightened out. Whenever a boss is capricious, lower executives should band together and form a network that enables them to carry on with business in spite of the whims of the man upstairs.

DO: Try to avoid such a syndrome in yourself by setting up a set of checks and balances. If you have a trusted colleague ask him or her to "monitor" you. I knew one very high-level exec whose secretary would put none-too-discreet bugs in his ear when he would start acting up—sort of like a conscience who could type 120 words per minute. Whatever works for you . . .

DON'T isolate yourself into the grandness of your position. It is one thing to insist that your people work out certain problems on their own; but you had best start opening up when you find nobody is talking to you about anything at all anymore. Again, strike a balance.

Firing Down Below

If you are looking for a good guilt trip, there is nothing that compares with the business of having to fire somebody. It makes no difference that the person may be incompetent, nasty, lazy, abrasive or downright unlikable; nobody likes to be in the position of being the one to terminate him. It touches everyone's own fear of losing his job, and there is always the superstition that God will punish you for it. He won't, but you may put yourself through so much guilt that you'll do it yourself.

Firing people is part of the job of being boss. If you aren't up to it, you should find some way to remove the onus from yourself by asking the personnel director to sit in with you or at least advise you. As I mentioned earlier, avoid moralizing. If you are taking this action with the right intention, if the person really must be let go for whatever reason, there is no need to agonize over it. Some business activities are unpleasant, but they have to be done or no business will transpire.

The correct way to terminate anyone's employment is in stages. If the person's performance is not up to par, you should have discussed the matter in detail with him and provided specific complaints and detailed how the various offenses should have been performed instead. If the person is being fired because of an attitude or a personality problem, you should have made it clear early on. You should always give the person at least six weeks to shape up before preparing a berth on the outgoing ship. You as a supervisor have the right to expect an immediate change in attitude at least, and a significant change within a week's time in the way a person is performing. The remaining period of grace is to see if the person has instituted a real change or is simply making a temporary accommodation.

We know of one executive who fired an employee after about eleven months' employment. He felt that he had given her a more than fair chance, but that she was not doing the job properly. She was a member of a minority and complained to the equal-employment-opportunity agency. Two years later the executive had to appear at a hearing to defend his action. Because of the legal complications that can arise these days in firing anyone, minority or not, many companies require managers to fulfill some rigid requirements before being allowed to fire someone. Needless to say, this leads to a lot of wasted time and frustration, having to cope with an unsatisfactory person until you make all the legal hurdles.

DO: Keep strong and accurate documentation of incidents that lead you to the decision to terminate an employee. Try, before coming into a job as boss, to have the company transfer people you feel you won't be able to work with. Where possible, take responsibility only for those people you hire or select from a previous staff.

DON'T give your ground too easily if challenged. You do have the right to demand competence from your staff. If someone is forced on you, demand that the person produce. There is nothing wrong with expecting top efficiency from the people who work with you. If someone wants a job so badly that he will go to court over it, he should be ready to work and work well.

Shooting Gallery

It is always difficult to fire people who have worked on staff for years before you take over. Even if it is absolutely necessary it can be a major stumbling block for the new person's success. If the staff has been a "small band," emotionally bonded to one another over a period of years, it becomes especially unfair. One particular example of this occurred when a beloved boss decided to move on to greener pastures, higher salaries and a career change. He had been very laissez-faire in his administration, allowing people to come and go as they pleased, allowing creative staffers to become influential. There were no definite hours as such, and they all had this close-knit family feeling, sharing one another's tears and joys, divorces and babies.

The new boss coming in had plans to revitalize the place, and he immediately met with resistance from his new staff. Some resisted him because he "wasn't Howard"—the person he replaced. Entrenched creative types who had set up little personal oligarchies were now devoid of clout, but fought his plans for change, even resorting to name-calling and mockery. One man even hung his picture with some uncomplimentary caption attached to it. Things got seamy for a while.

People who were used to wandering into work midmorning for the past eight years suddenly were expected to be at planning meetings at an early hour. The secretary who had typed letters when the mood struck was suddenly ordered to file her nailfile and produce a clacking noise. The outrage was intense. Surveying the scene, the new man realized he could keep only about three of the twelve, and these were lower-level people. It took years before he was able to finally reassemble a staff of bright creatives, and it was a struggle that came close to damaging his career.

By the time he finished he had lost a lot of clout with the company's management, whose members wondered why he couldn't pull things out of the hat immediately. (There was a movement to replace him, but a powerful friend deferred it.) The strain of keeping up production while replacing people who resent you can be devastating.

There are two ways to approach such a situation. The best is to bring in a very strong associate to implement your new ideas while you handle the diplomatic areas and search for new people. Often two new leaders can fire up the old staff with their enthusiasm and achieve their plans without major restructuring. A team of people gives off a sort of energy field which is more attractive and has more validity on a psychological level than a single upstart who comes in with a lot of funny zeal.

The other way is not to come on as the great reformer. People in business hate that sort of thing. As a lone person it is best to implement your ideas quietly, replacing select people while appearing not to be carrying out a jihad. Simply appear as though you are joining the staff and work from within to make your changes. The changes can be major, but there's where your clout as new boss comes into play.

DO: Get to know your people as soon as possible so that you will know who is most likely to remain. Try to retain as much of the old staff as possible, since training replacements is a draining business. Give the ones who are to be terminated a running chance by informing them as early as possible that you plan to replace them. Reassure the ones who are to stay that they are secure.

DO: Ask members of the staff what they feel should be changed. Very often when changes are necessary there are people already on staff who are most willing to be a part of them.

DON'T lie. One person I knew actually lied to people, telling them they were secure when he was already interviewing to replace them. This is brutal.

DON'T tell everything. It isn't likely you even know everything you will do. Retain a certain aloofness about discussing many of your intangible plans.

Trust to Dust

One of the basics of good management is this: if you can't trust someone who works for you, get rid of him. Don't try to reform the person. He is a danger to you. If you don't do it early he may gain enough clout to place you in an embarrassing situation where it will be impossible to fire him, or very difficult. Then you'll learn the true meaning of Maalox.

We were told of one young executive who tried to be Mr. Nice Guy to a superambitious staffer who, as it happened, would stop at nothing to achieve his ends. "My mistake was in letting him get a toehold even though I sensed his animosity. I wanted to be fair. You can't do that with such people. I should have given him one counseling session, warned him I was onto him, and fired him immediately after the next offense."

In this case the executive had to travel a lot. While he was gone the staffer had opportunities to discredit him, since he had direct contact with the executive's boss. "He would give me insufficient or incomplete information when I'd return, so I was trying to work on a false premise." The area here involved banking computer research. "Since he had direct access to my boss, he made friends and impressed him, so firing him became a problem—I had to justify it. I did it finally, but I swallowed a lot of antacid along the way."

DO: Insist that any communication between your people and your higher-ups be done in written form, and make sure you are provided with duplicates. Keep them in the same place you keep Grandpa's gold watch. This will inhibit any funny business. And you will have nice documentation on hand to prove your points.

DON'T hesitate to vocalize your reservations about any people who must have direct contact with your boss. This psychological ploy will defuse any attempt on the part of your staffer to ingratiate himself with your boss. When it is time to proclaim his merits and get him a promotion, you can delineate his good points.

Will You Please Look Busy?

I looked out of my office at what was a typical scene among our staff: The editorial assistant was typing up some letters, peering through those strange eyeglasses made of black screens with holes punched in them that were supposed to improve her eyesight. My associate editor was lolled back in her chair like a Jewish mermaid, her legs crossed, dreamily smoking a cigarette and waiting for her prince to come. The copy editor was on the phone to her mother. The mermaid caught my eye and smiled and waved. I burst out laughing. I wondered how we ever met a deadline, but we always were well within the limits and the stuff was good. The only one who ever "looked busy" was the editorial assistant, and that was because she liked to get her work done so that she could work on personal items without interfering with the job.

If I walked down the hall to the accounting department there was a sort of sanctum-sanctorum effect, something like monks in the abbey illuminating manuscripts. Everyone's head was bent over a calculator, papers or something. Everyone looked so busy I felt I should walk on tiptoe and speak in hushed whispers to the petty-cash lady.

Whether or not your people should "look busy" depends on two things: (1) they are busy; (2) they do the kind of work that keeps them looking busy. The reason our editorial assistant looked busy was because her kind of work required constant caressing of typewriter keys. The associate editor needed to sit back and reflect on the manuscript that was in such bad shape that she virtually had to rethink and rewrite it. She could go mad—not to mention growing a hump—if she had to bend over manuscripts eight hours a day nonstop. I don't know what the repercussions would have been if we had put an embargo on calls to the copy editor's mother.

A smart boss does not raise hell with his people because they do not look busy. A good boss knows by the completed work and by his deadline schedule whether or not his people are working efficiently. I was told of one vice-president of a small company who did this sort of thing: Three people were standing around one person's desk and were discussing a project they were working on. The vice-president walked by, saw them and immediately went into his office and called them all in on the carpet—or the vinyl tile, I'm not sure of the décor. He read them out for hanging around the office talking about "nothing" when there was work to do. When he was told they were indeed talking about work they were doing, he didn't have the guts to swallow his mistake but accused them of lying.

DO: Exhibit a sense of knowledge about how procedures proceed in your own line of work—and in your own office. If you can't tell what people look like when they're working in your own business, have your eyes checked.

DON'T go on rampages. It makes you look like a horse's neck. One of the worst things a boss can do is make a scene—and worse, a scene over the work habits of people who are working well overall. It comes as an outrage to them, spoils their focus, wrecks their enthusiasm, and destroys your own clout as an effective manager.

Bad Bosses

Basically a bad boss is one who hurts the careers of his people and makes their jobs invalid in some way. A bad boss may in fact be a teddy bear, while a good boss may be unlikable and unliked. When you are making your decision about how to approach bosshood, the one factor to bear in mind is not to cut down on a person's skills, or abilities, or to provide less of an opportunity for growth than is possible. You may not be the kind of person who is a bundle of cheer or who has a ready wit and a disarming manner; you may make mistakes in diplomacy or not be ready to back up requests for raises; but as long as you provide a place where your people can work and express their talents to the fullest your company will allow, you can be considered a good boss.

The Putdown Boss

This is the boss who sees the talents of someone who works for him and, instead of helping the person gain an awareness of the fact, spends time making subtle derogatory remarks that undercut a person's self-confidence. Many bosses take this tack for two reasons: to keep a talented employee from leaving or trying to get more money; or to take credit for the person's work because the boss has no self-confidence. There is no reason for this approach, since talented people will be more willing to work for people who appreciate and bolster them, and the boss will get better results and more recognition if he gives them their due.

DO: Respect people's egos. Remember to respect your people as adults and colleagues. You are their boss to make things function better; put-down tactics make things function worse.

DON'T lose sight of the fact that you can be made to look bad when your staff doesn't work well.

The "You're Fired" Boss

I knew of two bosses of this kind. One purposely threatened on a regular basis to fire someone because she believed it was a way to gain control. The other one did it as a joke, but also to remind himself that he was the boss. For the latter it was like sucking a lemon drop and enjoying the constant flavor in his mouth. In both cases the effect was the same; no one took either of them seriously, and when people actually did leave, or they had to fire them, the bosses were the ones who were most upset, not the person on the way out. This is a foolish approach. It reveals you as an insecure boss who doesn't have the talent to maintain control in any intelligent way. People are not so scared that they can't see through such a transparent ploy. It is also annoying to the adults who are working for you to have such a childish, cheap thing laid on them regularly. It makes one wonder if you received your leadership training from an old Superman comic book.

DO: Note that both these people were fired themselves in manners that were humiliating and gossiped about widely. Neither ever recovered a position of power.

DON'T imagine that such obnoxious behavior is taken lightly, even if you think you mean it as a joke. Never joke about this area. People resent it deeply.

The "Flat No" Boss

A boss who is inflexible is a bad boss. A staff of people is in fact a unit of various ideas, plans, dreams and talent. The boss who makes dogmatic judgments, refuses to hear discussion about things, and won't ask for suggestions from his staff is a bad boss. A company is a cooperative affair. A boss has the responsibility for making final decisions, but he also has the responsibility to utilize the talents that his company is paying for. An inflexible boss is harmful to both the company and the people who work for him.

> **DO:** See yourself as a coordinator of ideas and of the people who have them. In many ways a boss is an approver and a counselor. By cutting people out arbitrarily you make it impossible for your company to grow.

> **DON'T** hesitate to find the merits in ideas and requests; and if there is a germ of an idea that can be developed, then ask that it be reworked with your suggestions. When you must refuse something flatly, do it with encouragement to continue thinking along the lines of generating new ideas.

The Timid Boss

Just as bad is the boss who can't say no. Either he doesn't trust his own judgment or he is afraid of being disliked. Either way the approach won't work. A boss is there to say when suggestions won't work, when people aren't working up to par, when people don't deserve raises—whenever anything needs a refusal. "No" is the most fearsome word in our language, of course, but there is no place in business for a boss who doesn't know the proper way to utilize it.

Sometimes the boss won't say no because his people are so talented and he doesn't want to stifle their creativity. As a result the people gain so much ascendancy that they turn into monsters and lose sight of the fact that they have someone over them. You should not let any single person gain so much clout on your staff that he or she dictates what should be your prerogatives.

> **DO:** Allow creative leeway, but limit the personal and egotistical excesses that you see developing.

DON'T hesitate to pull rank, even though it scares the hell out of you to do so. Do it by memo when your courage fails you.

The Boss Can't Take It

Many people are fine until they get to be boss. Then their insecurities hit: being in charge scares the devil out of them. They hide in the office. They duck out of meetings for "other meetings." They take drastic actions, such as making a sweeping decision to fire someone valuable, rather than pace out the problem and find a solution. They are too insecure to face working with problems; they can only deal in sweeping measures that eliminate people. They are scared.

Such a boss will never take an action about chronic problems in the office. He is impossible to talk to about raises, complaints, promotions. Problems are brought to his doorstep: they just lie there, then they die there. Sometimes his staff will take a positive action and provide him with answers, which he may or may not seize on. Usually things float and float. People become glum; people who should be kept on are fired. And he hides out while things go along at mediocre levels of efficiency.

DO: Face your insecurities. Every boss must encounter a period of adjustment. Learn how to cope with authority. The basic rule is to listen, ask questions of your staff, and take advice when you're in doubt. And allow yourself to make mistakes. The insecurity often rises out of a sense that you are not allowed to err. You certainly have that prerogative. If you make a mistake, just correct it.

DON'T avoid taking action just because you aren't sure of the outcome. This assurance comes out of experience.

The Guesswork Boss

There are people who become bosses who think there is only one way to arrive at quality: their way. A famous example is the story of Henry Kissinger, who kept sending a speech back to a writer to try to make it better. After several rewrites the frustrated writer caved in and said, "Mr. Kissinger, I can't do anything more with it." Kissinger supposedly replied, "Very well, I'll read it, then."

This is amusing, but working for such a person in business would be a study in hiding the knives and all blunt instruments. The attitude implies that you really think your people are lazy or not able to arrive at an acceptable final product within a human time frame. It keeps people in an unnecessary state of tension and frustration, so you may not actually get their best work. Some people work very fast; others must run things through a sifter time after time until they get the best product. It is the responsibility of a boss to be able to gauge what kind of person works for him.

Needless to say, it was rather careless of the speechwriter not to ask if there were any specific points that his employer wanted changed, or if there were any points that he wanted developed further. A good boss will try to save time and not drain his employees uselessly. He will avoid guessing games. If you have complaints, specify them, clearly and in order. If you want something changed, let the people know. If you are rejecting a total product, say why. The worst kind of boss is one who flings things back at employees and says, "This is terrible! Change it!" and walks away refusing to discuss it.

DO: Communicate directly your objectives and objections, so that your employees will know what you want next time.

DON'T sacrifice the peace of mind of your employees to play silly little games.

The Alcoholic Boss

Many corporations these days must deal with the problem of alcoholism or drug dependency among their executives. Some companies have set up recovery programs to help these people rather than fire them. This humane approach is laudable; it is not fair, however, to ask a staff of people to work under a boss who is not taking steps to solve his problem. The company may wish to hold on to the talents of the person, but the person may be nonfunctioning much of the time. People working under an alcoholic boss experience the same resentments, flashes of disgust and hatred that the spouse of an alcoholic goes through—also a lot of the same guilt because of these uncharitable feelings.

If you have problems with the bottle and are starting to get questions about it, you will probably go through outraged responses denying that you have a problem. You may also try to convince yourself that even though you drink a lot, you are functioning at top capacity on the job.

DO: Listen to what people are telling you. Do seek help from the company if it is available, without shame. Everyone has something he or she would rather not discuss, but alcoholism is one of the "acceptable" *bêtes noires*.

DON'T expect your staff to cover for you if you won't take the steps to overcome or at least admit your problem. Don't berate yourself for having a problem. Just find some way to cope with it and function on the job.

Points to Remember

Everybody has some problems being a boss. There is no such thing as a perfect boss. Perhaps there shouldn't be. Just bring yourself into the best focus possible and remember that good intentions are as important to being a boss as any other quality.

Anyone who works can make up his or her own list of kinds of bad bosses. In every case the criterion will be the same; the boss doesn't provide an atmosphere in which his staff can do their work at optimum levels.

If you have been given authority over people in the place where they make their livings, and where they express themselves before their fellow workers, you have a responsibility to use all your capabilities. In ancient Greece bad leaders were thrown off the side of a cliff when they exhibited incompetence. In America, it seems, they're always kicked upstairs.

Finding People

A new boss may run into problems when it comes time to hire people to work under him. It is a good policy to hire known quantities when you are first learning this area of administration. The most successful hirings made by young people come from recommendations either within the company or through someone who knows what the person is like and can bring someone who will work well with the hiring party.

When hiring cold, either from unsolicited resumés, from newspaper ads or even from employment agencies, you are running into risks unless you have a particularly good sense of evaluating how people will act in future situations. As an inexperienced employer, you would do well to rely on people who know what they are doing. If you have a personnel department, turn to them for guidance and bodies. The personnel people generally know how to screen applicants, weed out whom you should not bother with, and send you people who have the experience and personalities that will combine with yours.

Judging the Resumé

I heard someone once say that when he gets a resumé that costs more than his shoes, he doesn't bother to follow up on it. Too many people try to compete by using resumés that are nothing more than overkill. I was once on a radio show where a mother called in and asked what she should do about her son. She said his resumé was too long. Since the show aired from four to six in the morning, it was obvious that she was worried sick about it. We weren't taking her seriously until I finally asked how long his resumé was. "Six pages!" she keened in frustration. "Who's going to read it?" Indeed, who would want to?

When going through resumés it is best to weed out first the ones that cloud the issue. I once received one that was comparable to a Milton Glaser graphic. A muted design on the two-toned paper made the high-quality printing less boring to read. None of your pedestrian Xerox machine—this was real letterpress stuff. It went on for three pages, and the man had been out of school for only two years. I'm sure I would have felt obligated to send him a wedding gift had I read the whole thing, it told me so much about him—and so little about what I was looking for in an editor. Since it is impossible for anyone of that age to have had much experience, I sensed he was trying to overcompensate for a natural state of affairs.

If you yourself are young, it is a good idea to aim your sights toward resumés that show some kinds of experience, even if it seems that the person doesn't have the direct experience you need. You are probably too young yourself to be training someone recently out of school who may not yet have a clear picture of where he or she wants to go careerwise. Let older and wiser bosses train them. You are in a scary enough position just training yourself. When looking at a resumé, seek this information:

• EXPERIENCE BACKGROUND. If the person appears to have run the company during his first year in the job market, remember that he probably had a lot of work to do. It's the new ones who carry the load of busy work. If he seems to have a heck of a lot of authority, the person is probably lying, unless he's a deposed crown prince.

• MISTAKES. If a person can't take the trouble to find a way to get you a resumé free of typographical errors, he isn't going to go to any great length to impress you once he's drawing pay.

• PATTERNS. These are visible in his extracurricular activities, or in the continuity of his background. If he shows a lot of changes in the kinds of jobs he's done, if there are lots of very short-term employments, you may or may not have an undependable here. A person's outside interests usually don't show what he will do on the job, but they will show whether or not this is a person who is interested in life. Remember that people who exhibit a lack of interest in the pleasures of life may be depressive. Or they may be workaholics. The second type may be just the ticket.

DO: Turn to the pros for help. A colleague with experience in hiring or a personnel supervisor will have an objective viewpoint of your own personality and be better able to match you up with someone you are most likely to get along with—not unlike computer dating.

DON'T screen resumés yourself unless you really have to. After the fifth one you will get to the point where you won't want to see any of them, or you'll be afraid not to see all of them.

Interview Chitchat

When you finally do chop and burn your way through the resumés and pick out some interviewees, prepare yourself before the first one gets there. Have on hand a list of things to tell the person, and a list of things to ask. You should take the lead, because the applicant won't have any questions to ask until he has more information. You, on the other hand, already have his resumé and the job description at your disposal.

Tell the person first what the job demands and what the duties will be. If you are starting something new, explain that much of the job will have to be defined by the person who will occupy it first. Remember that many people are not good talkers when they are in a pressurized situation such as a job interview. Try to gauge their interest. If the person asks questions and answers them, but is too shy to elaborate a lot, the person is worth a follow-up. If the applicant is just bored, sits and waits for you to make an offer just because she's there, it is advisable to terminate the interview with a thank-you and no promise of a follow-up. My favorite drip was a young woman who had done something "interesting" and was riding on that. She had worked on location with the film *Jesus Christ Superstar* and figured that that gave her more than enough clout so she didn't have to do any talking. I had the feeling she had presented herself only to be told when she should start. She made a nasty grimace when I terminated the interview with the statement that I wanted to "see more people."

One should expect to feel some warmth for and from a person. You should also remember that the position you are interviewing for has various requirements. If you need an outgoing person to deal with people as much as you do, it isn't likely you should hire someone who is shy at an interview. If the person is going to be an in-office deskbound helper who deals almost always with you, and you like the person, then investigate further.

When asking the applicant questions, try to keep things along lines that will let him open up. Don't start with a confrontation question like "Why did you leave your last job?" Ask first if he thinks he would like to do the job you just described. Then what kind of things he did that would lead him to do the job well for you. Try to get a picture of what his career goals are and what he wants from the future.

If he asks about the company, growth opportunities, possibilities of advancement, you may have a hot property here. Don't ask how much money the applicant wants for the job. State honestly how much you are offering. If he asks for more and you feel you can give it—and he deserves it—then scale up the offer. It's always best to settle money at the start rather than make half-promises of more in the future. Be as fair as possible so that there won't be *that* resentment to deal with during those important first months. If you can't pay more, say so. If the person wants the job, he should take it for the money that's there at the start, period. You as an employer must realize that it is impractical to expect someone to change jobs for the same amount of money. He may be giving up a sure thing for a flyer. You are morally bound to up his salary if he is going to risk changing jobs for one that may not pan out.

Remember that some people who are eminently suitable for a job can't sell themselves at all at an interview. If you can see through the shyness to the quality, you may find someone who will open up and grow beautifully into a job. Such people are apt to stay with you, since they are so shy about interviews.

Do's and don'ts to bear in mind when interviewing people:

• DON'T HIRE ANYONE on the basis of just one interview, unless there is no doubt at all that the dazzler is absolutely right. Hiring an employee is like buying a car: don't buy the first one you see.

• RECOMMENDATIONS FROM PEOPLE you know are usually solid bets, especially if the person referring is someone who knows your personality. Don't defer such an advantage. Someone coming in on such a referral is most likely to be him- or herself, since much of the shyness is removed.

• HAVE THE SECOND interview in a new setting. The first can be in the office; make the second one at lunch to see how the person acts in another situation.

• TRY TO HAVE a meeting with a third party present to get an even clearer picture of the person you are considering.

• SEPARATE YOUR EMOTIONS. You may find yourself bowled over by someone's aura, personality, energy, what-have-you. It may be that the person is absolutely right for the job, or it may be that you have been seduced by a personality. Bedroom eyes do not an employee make.

• IF YOU HAVE a nagging doubt about someone, don't make an offer.

• DON'T COMPENSATE FOR the applicant if the interview isn't going well. You will have to work with this person, and if your energies aren't naturally in sync they probably won't get that way later. If someone isn't putting forth a good effort at an interview, don't try to fill in the blanks because you are tired of interviewing, or because you sympathize with the person. Let the applicant put forth something special if she or he wants the job, even if something special is a special kind of charming shyness.

Gut Reactions

After all the scientific ways of hiring are gone through, the one real thing that makes the difference is your gut reaction to the person you are considering. Sometimes you will know that someone is right to work for you. There will not be that nagging doubt. It will come through loud and clear. But try to separate mental evaluations from your emotional reactions. If you are highly susceptible to, say, physical or sexual charms, don't use those as the basis for your gut reaction. The gut reaction is an intangible. You have a feeling of happiness, of rightness about the person in relation to the job. The resumé points may or may not be just right, but you feel that the person is. Think carefully before you run with it.

Don't hire anyone because you need someone right away—a body, *any* body—or because you hate to interview. If that is the case, get someone else to hire someone for you. If you keep hiring wrong people you'll never get any work done. And what a reputation you'll get! We know of one top-level female exec who can't get a secretary to work for her even at $500 a week because she has such a rotten reputation of being a monster to work for. You don't want that to happen to you. Take the careful route.

A Heartbeat Away . . .

Every good manager replaces himself at some point. If you are young and healthy and full of vitamin C, and you plan to stick around the old homestead awhile, then it is not so imperative to have someone ready to take over for you. The job is considered "yours" for a long time to come. It would be illogical to think that all situations remain static forever, though, so you should have a good backup, for your own peace of mind if nothing else. Everyone likes to get away. Only the most insecure want to be depended on so heavily that they can't take a vacation without worrying about the place not functioning without them.

Some corporations make executive promotion contingent on there being someone to replace the person moving up. It is part of executive competence to be able to hire and train people to take over eventually. By not allowing this situation, you may be viewed as not having any confidence that you will move up again; as having insecurity about your own talents; or as using a ploy to hold a gun to the heads of higher management if you are fired.

It is the mark of a professional to be able to identify one's successor—and even more of a credit to that executive if the person turns out to be excellent. This is accomplished through hiring good junior people, and by developing a staff that is so thoroughly aware of how the department functions that it runs smoothly under their competent direction. Except for certain kinds of decisions, any staff should be able to run for a few weeks without the presence of the boss. There may not be any innovations during that period, and there may be some fast discussion about emergency decisions, but that is definitely part of the plan.

DO: When moving out of the company, recommend someone to replace you, from your staff if possible. This is a courtesy, but also an affirmation that you have done an admirable job of hiring and training.

DON'T recommend anyone who will reflect badly on you, just because the person worked for you.

Hands Off!

There is an old phrase that sums up why you should not embark on the seas of love with people who work for you. Since it isn't a *nice* phrase, we won't utilize it here, but you get the drift.

Cartoons out of the old *Esquire* magazine, and the more recent *Playboy* humor, treat sex in the office as a joke or a romp or see it as an extremely light matter. It is not any of those things. It may be fun, but it is no joke. Do not have affairs with the people who work for you. Do not have them with the people you work with, either. The office should never be used as a sexual stamping ground.

It is usually the most talented people who get caught in the trap of thinking that they can carry on romantically—or sexually—with the people they work with, and in almost every case one or both gets fired or has to resign. The executives' graveyard is filled with the bones of affairs that backfired. The talented people usually figure that no one will find out because they are too clever to flaunt it. Ridiculous. The office is a fishbowl, and no one has any secrets of this kind. Someone always can pick up on the fact that two people are involved with each other, simply because you can't help relating in certain ways that any office yenta who's ever been in love can plainly read—out loud.

One major reason office dalliances can't work is that if your lover is talented you will be accused of favoritism when he or she gets raises and promotions. If you withhold raises and promotions in order to protect the affair from discovery, you are wrecking the person's career. If you become deluded into thinking the person is more talented than he or she is, you may promote the lover faster than is correct and someone else's career will suffer for it—someone, perhaps, who deserves the credit more than your lover.

When the affair is over, you will want to get rid of the person. You will not trust him or her to keep the past secret. You are vulnerable to blackmail, and your judgment is impaired. Often this mistrust is based on a very real resentment on the part of the ex-lover.

I once worked with a boss who hired someone who was very deserving of the job and did it brilliantly. Their affair started the day of the second job interview. What my boss didn't know was that his new lover also was a nasty, grasping, demanding person, aside from being brilliant at the job. If the lover did not have the clout of being the boss's Own, she would have had to contain some of the youthful brashness that made her so difficult to work with. Within a month the affair had been discovered, and within a year the monster whom Cupid had created was out of a job—and a lover. The boss lost a potentially excellent staff person and didn't have that good an affair either, he admitted one day. Along the way the person had upset everyone in some way or another, incited quarrels, and placed the boss in the position of constantly having to mediate or defend one or another of his staff.

> **DO:** Remember, no one is that good in bed that you need jeopardize a whole working staff to get involved. If you disagree, then your sexual focus is stronger than your career focus and it will be bye-bye to you early on.
>
> **DON'T** do it.

Two Bosses

In my early career I had two similar jobs within two years, under two different kinds of bosses. One was a man who was fair, a gentleman, and who expressed a strong positive attitude toward my work. After I went to work for the second one, a woman who was noted for being uncooperative and hell to work with, I thought I had made a terrible mistake. It wasn't until I left that job that I saw she was in fact the better boss. Despite her bad temper and intolerable mouth, she taught me the whole basis of what I needed for moving into a highly desirable job later on. She wouldn't take less than perfection. I should have known at the first interview when I showed her a copy of my first magazine. She opened a page and caught a glaring mistake that I had missed, that my first boss had missed and which was embarrassing. But she was able to evaluate me fairly nonetheless, and even provided a reason why the error existed. "I assume that's because you're doing it all yourself," she said, glaring at me from behind her huge glasses. I nodded in agreement. I was young, but not suicidal.

From the first day she wouldn't take anything less than perfection. She drove me crazy, but I learned what the business was really about fast, and she would call on me years later when she was "between associates." The first boss I had was courteous, considerate, a gentleman and lazy; I didn't like him. The woman was argumentative, domineering, impossible; I think of her often, fondly.

The personality of a boss is a variable that employees have to work around. A boss can be a pain in the neck, but everyone has to pay dues; it's better to pay them to a person who provides some decent compensation and lets his people develop a resumé that can get good jobs later.

Whatever kind of personality you have, as a boss you should focus on giving people your best shot on a professional level. You aren't in a personality contest, although there is never any reason to indulge yourself in temper tantrums and make life miserable for people. But if you can't control your emotions, at least make up for it where it counts the most. Give people a chance to grow.

Peering into Peer Groups

"Some people **are** *more equal than others."*

WHEN DEALING NECK to neck and dagger to dagger with people at your own level in the company's hierarchy, you must be aware of the diffuse ways in which power is displayed. At this level you must get what you want and need through various political maneuverings. This may take the form of alliances, friendships, one-upmanship, performing better than anyone else, or having a mentor who will give you everything you ask for.

Whatever the state of your personal clout, you still have to deal with your peers on what might be called an inner level. There is no way you can perform without being vulnerable to them on a psychological level. You may not need them to achieve specific goals, but you cannot divorce yourself from your basic psychological need for their approval. Even when you don't like someone, your natural reaction is to feel rejected if you find out that that person doesn't like you as well. People can train themselves not to be affected—or not to have their actions affected—by this basic need for peer approval, but the automatic response is there.

Part of this peer presence is identifiable in the control that a group exerts to keep individual members from departing from established patterns. Most peer groups are uncomfortable with anyone who "goes maverick" by exhibiting some original concepts away from the established repertory. It's okay to come up with ideas within a certain framework, but your group will feel very uneasy with radically new ideas. Of course, if you do get these new ideas going and they are a big hit with the public, then the peer group starts trying to imitate you. The key here is to gain so much clout through support from upper management that you set the standards for your particular peer group.

Some people create this aura around themselves by starting out "different," or entering the company as a bright new kid from the start. Then that person's radical ideas are part of what's accepted from him or her, and no one tries to bury them. The person's whole clout depends on being an original thinker.

Always remember when dealing with your peers that you are in a survival situation. During the early years too much of your future is undetermined and it's impossible to predict what survival tactics a colleague will adopt to claw his way to the top. It's easy when you're all young and have your whole future ahead, full of hope that you all will make it to the top together. When you start getting into the narrower opportunities of middle-level positions, then upper-level positions, you may start rummaging for your poison ring.

The thing to remember during heavy interaction with your peers is not to lose sight of your career focus. When you have to start politicking and competing for positions, it's easy to get lost in the melee of backstabbing, jealousies, hatreds, friendships and frustrations. It's during this time you must discipline yourself most severely and keep your perspective on what you are really in the competition for. Many people become soured by the constant tension-inducing squabbles that go on seemingly day by day. The negativity seems to outweigh the rewards. Many people who find themselves pushed out will breathe a grateful sigh of relief and vow never to go back into the corporate structure. A lot of sensitive people are lost this way.

It isn't necessary to give up on corporate life. It is easy to pick up on the negativity around you and begin to think it's the standard for corporate behavior. When a group of people becomes trapped into a negative way of thinking, they look for incidents to reinforce the truth of this negativity. It becomes The Way Things Are.

The real leaders are the ones who come up with ways to change the situation, rather than reinforcing it. Take positive steps to change the atmosphere, and start by controlling your own reactions and attitudes.

Building Power

The formation and use of power is an inexact science. You're dealing with human responses, and you must develop a sense of which spontaneous action will produce the desired response. Power is built in good part by thinking on your feet, like a boxer. To move ahead in business, you must become a psychological athlete. You must learn to respond automatically and spontaneously but still play by the rules of the game. To do this you have to know how to read the motivations of the people around you.

Example: One of your peers is extremely thrifty about things like picking up the tab for lunch, laundry, and small items that make daily life comfortable, yet he is always talking about investments. Such a person will probably do anything to cultivate professional friends. He is obviously money-oriented. By offering him a business alliance you will find a willing colleague, because he will see it as a way to increase his monetary worth. But don't depend on him to give anything extra in return.

You would use such a person only in a business situation where his money expertise can be shared for both your advantages.

If you work with someone who talks about "skirts" all the time, you can assume that this person operates on an emotional and physical level. He probably focuses more on the creative parts of his job. Such people are usually so taken with the pleasures of life they will do anything to expand the creative horizons around them. They usually are not backstabbers, being more concerned with their personal aesthetic needs.

If someone around you talks about his unhappy childhood and how dull and lonely it was, you can be sure this person's need for security and position will make him stop at nothing to achieve it. You must watch this type like a hawk, since the time may come when he will resort to something underhanded.

If someone who works for you cannot accept praise or honest expressions of credit, yet is an excellent worker, he will probably never give you any reason to doubt his loyalty to the job, or even to you. As long as you reinforce his sense of worthlessness by not talking about how good he is, he will appreciate you.

It is important to remember that people's actions are rooted in basic personality traits that almost always remain constant. There is no such thing, for example, as someone stabbing just one person in the back. There is no such thing as lying about just one incident. It is important to get a hook on the motivations of each of your colleagues and determine in which areas they can be trusted and work from there.

DO: Keep your eyes open for signals to true motivating factors.

DON'T play psychiatrist. If someone has a problem, work around it or with it, but don't get involved in it.

Whose Job Is This, Anyhow?

It is important for you to define your territory. When someone else starts doing a project that legitimately should be done by you, then you must make things clear to that person. Your job responsibilities should have been defined before you even agreed to take the position in the first place. This should have been agreed upon by you and your boss at the start. All duties and responsibilities and authority should have been clearly stated, and even written down, so that there would be no mistake.

Sometimes a peer steps in by accident; sometimes your boss may assign to one of your colleagues a project that legitimately should have been given to you. At these times you must step forward and confront the peer and/or the boss. In either case the peer must be confronted. It is necessary to confront the boss only if he has had a direct hand in the oversight.

Confront your peer calmly. It will serve no useful purpose to storm into someone's office and lay it waste in anger when someone steps into your territory. First, ask for the facts; second, ask if the person is aware that this area comes under your jurisdiction; then inform the person that in the future he or she must discuss the project with you to determine who will conduct it. If you meet with scorn, if the other person tries to shame you out of your rights by indicating that you are acting childishly, stay composed. Assure the person that you have no problem sharing the company, but you will not be able to function at your best capacity if you do not know everything that is going on. Explain that the matter has been placed under your supervision, and insist that you oversee the project this person has started. If the person refuses, then you can register a more strenuous objection in memo to your own boss. Before doing that, make sure you have sent a memo to the transgressor so that there is no mistake about who said what.

It happens sometimes that people who have little in the way of business smarts will unwittingly offend in this way and back off quickly and politely, with apologies, when informed of their mistake. However, some people just don't respect the territory of others, and may be intentionally stepping into your job and taking a bite out of the material that you intend to use to fashion your clout. Such a one must be made to step back.

Sometimes people may try to utilize (or brutalize) the people who report to you. I had such a problem when I was at one company. I discovered my associate, a woman about twenty-four, typing up something I didn't recognize. I asked her what it was. She said the company head's new golden boy had come in and told her to type it. I removed it from her typewriter, took it to the G.B. and told him that he was not to give assignments to people on my staff. If he wanted something typed, I informed him, without smiling, the company provided a receptionist who also doubled as backup typist when things became jammed.

He said he had assumed it was all right, since my associate worked in the same company. I pointed out that we were in a separate office—with a closed door—and that in any event my associate, though young, pretty and a woman, was not a secretary, nor even a very good typist. By way of apology he asked why nobody had told him. I said that nobody expected him to do such an outrageous thing and, finally, smiled and departed.

It is essential to define your boundaries and to do so correctly. In the above example it was also necessary for me to tell the people on my staff that nobody was to give them any assignment except me, and that if anyone tried they were to refer the intruder to me.

DO: Be gentle if possible, yet firm, and always composed. If the intruder has so little business awareness as to consider overstepping in a matter of no importance, you can rest assured such a person won't make it when the competition becomes a crunch. If the offender is your boss, your complaint must be strongly expressed, and you should be ready to stand up for your prerogatives.

DON'T bring the matter to your boss unless it becomes clear you can't handle it yourself. If you feel your boss won't back you up, it may even be better to forfeit one battle. If you must forfeit this single battle, strike out and find ways to strengthen your position in such a way that you will have too much clout for it to happen again.

DON'T blow up and lose the battle that way. An air of unexpressed indignation or dismay should back up your words.

The Power Look

Your personal image, created by the clothes you wear, the visual impact you make, is an essential tool for achieving your career goals. The style you get as an executive can either alienate, intimidate or soothe your colleagues. Sometimes, of course, your image is dictated by the type of profession you are in. People dealing with the law or with banking are required to dress in conservative clothing that portrays their ability to dress expensively and partake of the extras involved in looking good—tailoring, accessories that are status symbols, and the kind of maintenance that keeps the clothes looking impressive.

In other fields, you may have more freedom to express your particular personality in a more individualistic way. You may or may not wear ties if you're a man; you may opt for pant suits or highly expressive clothes and styles if you're a woman.

I knew one tough cookie of a woman executive who had achieved a lot of clout and position—and money—in a fairly short time. Her look, even at forty, was distinctly demure. I was talking about her to someone who knew her and he was commenting on how someone so young had achieved so much. When I told him she was well past her third decade he was floored. She always looked quiet, nice, and young. And she was the toughest executive I'd ever met. Since she worked in a male-dominated industry, she had automatically assumed an image that she knew was not threatening to her peers, and made it work.

If you want to affect the style of an *enfant terrible,* you may want some extra dash and flair in your clothes—an image that makes it look as if you had spent a lot on clothes but didn't much care how eccentrically you put them together in the morning. Quirky combinations, like a sport coat, a button-down collar, no tie, and casual slacks, or even, at times, designer jeans, with a trenchcoat piled on top of it all as an afterthought—such would carry out your image.

If you want to intimidate, wearing total outfits such as a dark pinstripe suit by a name designer—tailored to within a pinstripe of its life—and carefully orchestrated accessories will leave your fellows feeling like wrapping the draperies around themselves when you're in the room. It's real upmanship to look good down to your toes, to flash a Corum watch without thinking of it—you're just thoughtfully touching your chin while your colleague talks to you. Because you *know* how to put together a look that works and he or she doesn't, because you manage to afford something the others can't, people are impressed. Whether you're male or female, develop some kind of strong, careful executive image. It will strengthen your position and make you stand out from the crowd.

Don't forget to put money into your hairstyle. Even if you don't pay much, make sure your hair is cut well and washed well and looks as though you have some sense of what it's doing on your head. Too many male executives will spend much money on suits but let their hair fly out at odd angles. Nothing is more exasperating than watching a man with a tangle of hair badly askew on his head while he's telling you how to handle your money or business affairs. If your hair is thinning, get a cut that facilitates the event; don't try to keep combing it into the preppie style you used when you were nineteen. Grow up and get a man's haircut.

Women at lower and middle levels should have cuts that indicate a certain seriousness about business. Some very successful women execs can manage a style that looks as though it needs special care, but most women on the way up should have a cut that looks as though it doesn't require much care to maintain. It provides a better focus on your talents and imparts more of an impression that you are more serious about your work than about your hair. As you move up, however, your impact is heightened by the fact that you can wear a more elegant style and have the time and money to maintain it. The impression then is that your hairstyle is as important as any other aspect of your career.

Role Acceptance

The head of any staff of any size must be aware that his or her actions will set the tone for that staff. One of the hardest things to accept is this kind of focus on one's personality. Most people want to sidestep it, do not feel adequate to the posture, are embarrassed by it. In reality this is a part of one's duties as boss, and probably one of the most important.

One must set aside one's ego and realize that it is false modesty to say, "I'm not the kind of person I want people to emulate." This is not the issue. You have become a leader; your bosses feel you have the ability to supervise; the people under you want you to set the style and make decisions about how they should operate. It has little to do with your private personality. The issue here is taking on the job of administration and making decisions that are correct for your staff and for your company—and for your own career as well, of course.

It's never too early to establish priorities in relationships. Two people who set up a department together cannot help but feel close during this time of birthing together. Close friendships may develop on a temporary basis. Remember that these are exactly that—temporary feelings based on that unique experience that no one else shares with the two of you. Expect things to develop away from that kinship eventually, despite the fact that you will probably always remain loyal and well disposed to each other. Some strong relationships are temporary—like pledges going through Hell Week together, New Yorkers during a blackout, and raising dachshund puppies together. The thing to remember is this: although you may be spending up to twelve hours a day with each other, eating and walking home together, you are still doing an office thing. When the stupendous need is over and things enter a more normal phase, you may both want to separate church and state again. Do so.

At this time of goodwill and energy-sharing it is still important to establish your image of department head with your secretary. And it is also important to make distinctions between your office demeanor toward your next in command and your secretary. If you want to maintain a certain separateness or aloofness from the office assistant, then you can arrange for her to take assignments from someone else. If you prefer to make the secretary more interwoven throughout all aspects of the department, eventually making this person a private secretary when the time comes, then you would arrange more direct communication lines.

It is always difficult in a small department of three or four people to try for aloofness of the department head. It leads to certain resentments and confusion of signals. The best course of action is not to pull the crowned-head act until much later, when your department grows large. Let nature take its course. You should allow the small-band atmosphere to prevail, while maintaining the fact that you are indeed the head of the small band. This is a great learning experience, being able to have this kind of intimate communication with each member of your staff, and you shouldn't let it pass by untouched. It will broaden your experience of being a leader. The idea of holding oneself aloof in these early situations for fear of laying the wrong groundwork is erroneous in itself. You will never have a better opportunity to have an insight into the way people's minds work at work. If you can get this experience it will help you "read" people at higher levels when the situations are more formalized and your colleagues do not express themselves so ingenuously.

Remember to keep open lines of communication with people at your peer level during times of taking over higher-level jobs. It's important to keep your bearings, and to remind yourself how to deal with "equals" in the corporate structure.

DO: Hire a second in command when you set up a new department. You'll need the support and loyalty.

DON'T be afraid to allow changes to occur in your relationships with people. As you grow and as your needs change, your business interactions will reflect those changes. Don't feel self-conscious or guilty about changing relationships.

The System

Some companies, particularly law offices, have a certain sacredness of hierarchy. Certain executives cannot be interrupted unless a matter has a certain importance; certain people dare not approach certain Olympian officers without damn good reason and credentials. This is the way things are, and we are not here to heckle and jibe. We are here only to warn young people who are new to corporate affairs that in some offices some people don't talk to other people unless spoken to or sent for. There is a chain of command and it takes on a certain air of Vatican or Buckingham Palace layering.

It always depends on the type of business you are in. If you work for a publishing house you may find yourself wisecracking with officers of the firm in the elevators or halls regularly as a matter of course. If you work in a law firm you may never see the senior partners except when their litters are carried by your office.

You must decide how you are going to handle being a boss in your own career. Not with the people above you, because that is already laid out for you. The people below you, who report to you, must have accessibility to you. You must decide how to handle that accessibility. Do you speak only to those people directly below you and let them deal with the assistants, or do you want a more direct approach so that you'll have a feel for the attitudes in your office? How democratic do you want to be, within the parameters set by your company as a whole?

Always remember that you should not buck the company decorum too extensively, even if you have a lot of clout. The people below you can have easy access to you without your flying in the face of The Way Things Are Around Here. Keep your dealings with your assistants, secretary and staff a departmental matter, even if you must tell your people not to discuss your leniencies with their contemporaries. For example, if you and your secretary have a high degree of rapport because of your adaptability, she at lunch with the other secretaries may rhapsodize about you when they start snarling about their bosses' intractabilities. This may then cause them to become disaffected and perhaps start comparing your methods favorably with their bosses'. Then you will get flack from *your* colleagues for making them look bad.

It does little good to suggest they improve their methods. Best to keep your little secret of success and not make enemies. Most people like to think that everyone should adapt to the lowest common denominator, not that everyone should welcome constructive criticism.

The big point here is that you must have good relations with your colleagues and maintain your image and standing with the senior officers. If your colleagues complain about you because you are making waves that disrupt the company morale, the senior officers are not going to go to the secretaries and ask who's right. It is best to maintain a sense of privacy when you know you are going against the stream.

If your fellow execs, however, come and ask you why your secretary is so efficient when they can't seem to lock onto the right track with theirs, you can certainly provide some advice and then gain in repute. But try to keep yourself from making serious offenses in the eyes of the people who can break you.

DO: Respect the patterns of power in your company. They may seem absurd to you, but obviously someone needs them or they wouldn't be there. In many ways such systems help people higher up focus on the points they need to concentrate on without having to deal with the confusing melee. If you can use it for yourself, then adopt its tenets.

DON'T buck the system like a rogue. It's to your own advantage to innovate changes in subtle ways that can be adopted by others who see that they may be improvements over the existing patterns.

Nice-Nice

There is an attitude of scorn these days about niceness: we have a tendency to think of it as tacky, to put it down. Cynicism is more respectable to many people, especially in the tough-tough world of business. Too bad. Like it or not, we have a built-in biological response to a smile. We like it. You still catch more flies with honey than with vinegar. Our emotional reactions respond to extremely simple stimuli. You smile; people want to work with you. You shout; they want to see you on unemployment. It's that simple.

However, the plasticized smile, seen through Lucite, doesn't work: the unrealistic manufactured brightness of an afternoon TV host; the person who thinks everything is unbelievably wonderful, fabulous, and hits these words with such mechanical vehemence they can't possibly support the illusion.

It is important to emit positive vibrations in a subtle way. You should utilize the accepted pleasantries with your staff and coworkers. It's one thing to cut corners financially; it is not advisable to cut out the little intros of life's day-to-day interactions. "Good morning," "how are you," and little pleasant anecdotes all make for a warmer correspondence between people. The person who starts right in talking to someone each morning as if an evening and a night's separation had not occurred is exhibiting a lack of caring that works in a subtle way. Most people are somewhat taken aback by this suddenness. It makes them feel they are not important on any level except the very specific business areas. Who wants to be a warm-blooded computer? One of the biggest complaints employees have against their bosses is basically this: the boss doesn't care about their sensibilities. All other gripes are an outgrowth of this basic point.

The need for business "graces" becomes even more pronounced when dealing with your peers. These people need not cope with many of your personality flaws and may even dislike you enough to work against you. The best tool you have in dealing with your peers is mutual respect and friendly cooperation.

DO unto others as you'd have them do unto you. The corporate graveyard is full of the bones and the ivories of people who have chosen to ignore this dictum.

DON'T trample on people who come to you offering personal consideration and a cooperative attitude.

Rivalry

Rivalry is often a healthy thing in an office, even if it does mean that two people may be in some competition with each other. When you are in a situation where a rival has more clout than you do it may be necessary to take steps to keep it from being used against you. One way is to place yourself in a position where your presence in a job is vital. This usually means working hard, which in turn increases your own clout.

People in competition in an executive situation don't have to turn against each other unless one is threatened by the other. When someone starts to work against you it is due to some kind of insecurity, and that fact alone gives you power if you want to use it. Nobody tries to oust a person who is not a threat. If someone is working against you in this way you must take security in the knowledge that you are powerful enough or talented enough to pose a threat to him.

When the Race Is Fixed

Several years ago a Grand Old Man at the head of a company that was nationally known and respected decided to retire from active leadership. He called in his two best executives and told them that he planned to choose his successor from the two of them. For the next year they would be in direct competition with each other and he would make his decision. Sounds like an old *Twilight Zone* rerun, but it happens to be true. The men were equally talented, in fact, and had always been highly useful to this company. The race was run and one was chosen, and, of course, the other was out. He went on to his own successes. The question is, did the Grand Old Man make a wise decision to call such a race?

On the face of it he did, since he got a wonderful successor who raised the company to even higher repute. But many people feel the Grand Old Man should have known by that time who the successor should have been without taking the chance of dividing his entire staff. The staff, seeing two possible choices, perhaps could have lined up behind one or the other of their possible future bosses. This could cause chaos and resentment when the successor was finally chosen.

Business, in fact, is a game of sorts, and only a very wise G.O.M. could have controlled the situation so that deep resentments were not built up during the time of contest.

Many bosses try to engender some sort of rivalry as a healthy competition to increase production, sales or creativity. Such incentives are desirable only as long as the rewards are based on normal compensations. Any boss must be careful how he sets up horseraces in the office. The larger the prize, the larger the risk of disaster. It is better nowadays to make your decisions and announce them than to put people under a war of nerves that may or may not pull the results you want.

Jealousy

Jealousy is both debilitating and destructive. You can never and should never compare the advances someone else has made in his career to your own. Some people are early starters, while others need much more time. Some people make a lot of money very early, while some others may not make much at thirty-five. You may know someone who is twenty-three and making $80,000 a year. You may suddenly ask yourself, What am I doing with my life? That person's large salary has nothing to do with what you are doing with your life. It is, after all, your life to do with what you please.

The difficulty arises when we view everything in terms of money and power. A career must be taken in a total sense. Your job must be seen not only as a tool for paying the rent and food bills and buying movie tickets, but also as a vehicle for your own personal development—your cultural or mental or spiritual growth, in a way. Our society makes it very difficult not to be blinded by our paychecks. Everything seems geared to pricing: your salary is a price; your house is an investment; your kids are deductible.

The pressures are very high on us all the time to maintain a certain income level or be embarrassed by it. We tend too much in corporate affairs to judge people by their salaries, and that makes people feel that they are not very successful if they make average incomes. None of this is very healthy, since it leads to depression and bad attitudes. We are in the midst of a serious imbalance in our evaluation of what is important in our lives, and this is nowhere more visible than in the way people approach their careers.

You must work very hard to maintain a sense of reality in your work. Many people will take a job they don't like all that well, because the money is hot. Others know that liking their jobs can provide similar compensation. If money is the only reason to work, then your life can become very stale and empty indeed. Money is the founding reason for people to work, but liking your work is important to keep from losing your human spirit.

DO: Develop a true sense of your own abilities, and rely on that security. If you need a constant answer to "How'm I doing?" you should ask your professional friends and boss for evaluations periodically.

DON'T be too hard on yourself at any point. The reason—partially anyway—for building a career is that you enjoy it. So enjoy it.

Discrediting

There arises a time—maybe many times—when discrediting becomes necessary. Usually it is when a co-worker is making a mess of things, you know it, and your own workload is increasing in a direct inverse ratio to his slackadaisical ways. If you cannot approach the co-worker directly or he's uncooperative, then it becomes necessary to go to the boss and present a list of grievances. Either the person shapes up or the person ships, as you may hope, out. This can be tricky business if it is the boss's fault that such an occasion arises and the put-upon co-worker must take this extreme and onerous responsibility of making the matter known at court.

Why is the person slacking off? Why doesn't the boss know or care?

If you find yourself in the position of having to present a complaint about a co-worker, you must have some solid facts to present with the complaint. If not, you can run the risk of becoming the guilty party. The boss may see you as a troublemaker who is trying to build a career on the reputations of others.

If you have a valid case it is sometimes a good idea to make the matter known for another reason than just getting your work done. If you are seeking advancement in the future and there is a real reason why you should get it over someone else, then this kind of situation can tip the scales in your favor. You should not make up a case against someone to destroy him, but you should not support someone passively if there's a possibility of seeing him promoted over you.

DO: Stay on the up and up when dealing with such situations. Make sure the situation truly warrants a complaint to the boss. Some minor matters should be handled between you and the offending co-worker. If you do it this way you may even build a loyalty for covering for him.

DON'T become a tattletale. By sticking to strictly professional tactics, and bringing only serious and righteous matters to the front, you will help your own credibility.

Confronting

There are right and wrong ways to confront your colleagues. One of my favorite wrong ways involved two women executives in what might be called a highly volatile creative area. Toward the end of the confrontation, which was held in the corridor outside their offices—Wrong Way Item No. 1—one screamed something in a foreign language to her co-worker. The other screamed back, "Not only are you the biggest whore-bleep in all of New York, but you speak the world's worst French!" To which the other replied, "Bleep you, and the dog you rode in on."

Clearly, the wrong approach, if an entertaining one.

The right way involves telling your colleague, in private, step by step, what your complaint is, and in which specific instances the fault has been observed. If you have been or feel you have been victimized by this person, you should say so and detail the specific instance. If you have some minor complaints, if the person is simply nudging you in the wrong way, then bring it into the open, leaving room for discussion. In fact, always make the confrontation an opportunity for an open exchange of talk about the matter that's on your mind.

Starting from Scratch: Setting Up Your Own Department

As far as power and clout and such psychological tangibles go, it is a lot easier to start your own brand-new department than to take over one that already exists. You set the tone for the action; you establish the rules and set the style. The problem is that you may be trying to materialize a dream. It is rather difficult sitting down to a blank sheet of paper and having to construct a whole department from scratch. Everything seems to lead back to nothing. You need a budget, but you won't know your budget until you know your costs, and you won't know your costs until you hire people and start projects, but you can't do that without knowing how much money you have. That's the way it feels, anyway.

You can always pattern your department on a previous one, of course. You should set up a list of things you want to accomplish, the equipment you'll need and how many people you expect to want to hire. It's usually a good idea to have someone in mind, or to hire someone whose abilities you can rely on to help you get organized. This person should be the first one you hire. You will need that person to bounce ideas off. Be sure he has a vested interest in the success of the operation, since he will probably end up in the position of next in command to you. Failing that, get yourself a super-duper secretary right off the bat and use your honeymoon clout to get her a decent salary. Then get ready for some deep-into-the-night meetings, plannings and hard work.

The reason it is preferable to have a higher-up chosen so soon is to determine how many other staff people you'll need and what functions they should be expected to fulfill. Some departments don't hire secretaries *per se,* but find it better to hire an assistant who can do clerical work as well. If you are doing this, be prepared for the quick eventuality of this person wanting more. If the person has goals other than doubling as a secretary, he or she will be campaigning for more responsibility—and later dunning you to find some other secretary to free her or him of these duties. When starting a new department, don't forget that time frames tend to go faster than you think. You should try to get someone who will remain a secretary for a minimum of three to five years.

Do not minimize the importance of a secretarial person either. Every department needs someone there to type things on a daily basis, to answer phones, to handle all those things that other staff members can't do. It is a bad idea to promise yourself that an assistant who doubles as a secretary will be able to move into other areas soon. When the time comes you will find that you don't need this person in that fantasy projection, but you very definitely need a secretary. Budget one in from the start, and leave possible vacancies of the future both vacant and in the future until you know what those job descriptions will be. Make it clear to your secretary that you expect her to remain a secretary.

> **DO:** Get as good a reading as possible on what kind of personnel requirements you are likely to have.
>
> **DON'T** be afraid to make required changes early. Sometimes you have to play the game for a while to see how to play it right.

Sweeping Clean: Taking Over a Department

When taking over a position that was held by someone else, it is a good idea to get a picture of what your predecessor did right and, more importantly, what the people you now work with think he did wrong. Without asking for complaints about the person, ask them how they feel the job has been carried out. They will be more than happy to fill you in on what he did wrong. These complaints will tell you just what sets your new colleagues off on a snit. Discuss with them suggestions for change that they feel will facilitate getting the job done smoothly.

Such a tactic will help you arrive at a better insight into how to do your new job. It will also provide you with unmatchable information on how to do the things you may not have been sure of or aware of. Remember that you won't get effective work out of your people if you repeat the mistakes of your predecessor. There are few things as alienating as a new broom that doesn't sweep anything.

> **DO:** Ask what methods didn't work. Which items were a direct hindrance. Suggestions for making things better. You may have more clout as a new person than the previous person did. Remember that companies expect to have to lay

out more money to back up a new administrator than they did for the old one.

DON'T hesitate to amend and rectify the old situation. You are expected to make changes. Don't feel obligated to follow everyone's suggestions —you are the one in charge, after all.

Further Conversations

Whether you are taking over an already existing department or starting a new one as its first supervisor, it is very helpful to meet with other established department people whom you will be dealing with in the future. From these people you can gain insight into deadlines, budget requirements and office procedures based on their needs and experience.

Such investigation can also help you get a reading on the personalities, moods and negative qualities of these people and find out what you will be up against early on.

During this time it is best to take the mendicant approach. Don't demand what you want; go to people asking what's available, then decide your future needs and ask for what you want at a subsequent meeting. Always remember that people can be made either to want to help you or to resent the extra work. It all depends on how things are presented to them. It is not likely that by respecting their sensibilities and egos you will raise their hackles. As a new kid on the block it is good sense to hold back on demanding, even if you have the clout to do so, and establish yourself as cooperative and considerate at the start. You may run into opposition from other departments, but if you handle it in a diplomatic way you will most likely disarm your adversaries and get what you want. Always remember what is important: getting what you want—not a momentary ego gratification. In business the one who has to be handled is the one who loses; the one who knows how to handle intractable people always comes out ahead.

DO: Use the opportunity to make friends. Do ask questions of them. Let people talk; some people may feel they have to assert themselves at the start, then become cooperative when they see that you intend to be.

DON'T be difficult. A soft answer turns away wrath. You may think that by being difficult or confrontive you are establishing power. In reality you are squelching an opportunity to learn things that may be vital to your future clout.

The Previous Occupant

Some executives are gracious in offering to share information and insights with the people who succeed them. Some won't tell you a thing. It is by no means essential to powwow with your predecessor, but it can be helpful.

Most new people prefer to establish a new order, especially if the previous administrator let things fall into disrepair. One new department head called his staff into the office one by one and told them each, "I want you to forget everything you did when E—— was here. I plan to start out on a totally new road." Since his predecessor had agreed to stay on an extra week to provide a transition period, it made things rather awkward.

In general it is more of a hindrance having a "twilight occupancy" of your new position, since it really delays the actuality of your assumption of power. If you can avoid such a situation, you will be better off. Soft, blurry edges when making such a change are not helpful to asserting your authority.

Avoid comparing yourself to the past person. Don't refer to him by name; don't join in discussions about him. If you want a reading on how he did things, ask him at the start, and thereafter ask about the *methods,* not about the person. Don't let him hang around in spirit. Place your own style on the job as quickly as possible.

One to One

When seeking information about how to do certain jobs involved in your new position, try to do it on a one-to-one basis. Don't display your ignorances at open meetings. It is required that you instill in everyone a sense of confidence that you can do the job. It will work against you psychologically if you display yourself as a total learner. Yes, everyone needs advice when taking over; that is acceptable. But don't ever place yourself in a public position of asking to be taught.

When seeking information, ask to have a "meeting" with the person from whom you need help. Present an image of a self-confident executive on a fact-finding tour, not of a green kid, gaga with confusion, looking for someone to head him in the right direction.

Don't forget that people love to display their expertise. Give them a chance to perform, and write down what they say, if you feel it is necessary. Some people feel that a good exec can absorb the information without the hook of a pen and a pad. It is probably good for making a power impression, but on the other hand you might forget it. Use your discretion.

Budget Budging

When establishing your budgets for a new department, you will undoubtedly be involved in meetings with people who don't want to give you any money. Find out what funds are actually available, set up your schedules realistically, and use your honeymoon clout to go after a little more. Always budget in an invisible employee, since every successful department will need to hire someone new within two years. If the money hasn't been allotted, you may have to run crippled for a while until you can get the green light to hire someone.

View your budget for a new department in the same way a new company views its seed money. You should have enough to back you up realistically for a number of years, which can be determined only by the current economy, the actual business you are in, and sales projections. You must also be realistic in your expectations. Try to get a good handle on what your company will expect from you in a certain time frame, and gauge that against what you feel you will be able to produce.

Try to get a budget that will place you on a level with other departments. It is not good to be unable to provide the salaries for your employees that are available in other sectors. Also use your new clout to get the money you need. The optimum time for obtaining what you want is exactly when you are setting up. Don't hesitate to ask for the "home environment" you need to work in. Office equipment, office space, décor, furnishings, should all be part of the budget.

Treading on Eggs

When you are taking over as head of an existing department many problems become pronouncedly those of the psyche. The organization is already there and has been functioning without you. It may even be that it has been functioning very well prior to your installation, and that the reason for the change in leadership was only that your predecessor moved on to better things. It may be that you were not brought on because the higher administration was dissatisfied—they may even want to maintain the status quo. Then your approach must follow a much narrower course.

Whenever you take over a position of leadership it is usually because the top people in the organization like you. They are well disposed and want to give you support. This is called the honeymoon period, and it is fragile. An early wrong move on your part can shift the mood over into distaste or annoyance and you will have to scrabble for lost ground. Generally speaking, if you have been brought in or promoted from within as a replacement for someone who has been doing the job admirably it isn't likely that you will have to worry much about losing favor, unless you make some monumental errors.

If you have been installed as a replacement for someone who

was doing a bad job, and who was fired or resigned in disgrace, you will be in an unenviable spotlight. You will probably be watched closely, and much will be expected of you to make fast improvements. Good luck.

The First Weeks

The mistakes you make at the start will dog you as a leader from that point. You may come in as the golden kid at the start, but your approach at this time will show whether or not that's just gold paint. The most visible example we have had of this in recent times was Gerald Ford. He came in with the promise to wash away the deep negativity that had settled over everyone because of Watergate. He was seen as a hope for a better climate. After only a short time he gave his predecessor a pardon, and the clouds came down again even stormier than before and he never regained the trust he had lost. This psychology works just as effectively at any level of leadership. You should not take a highly controversial step without first establishing your style and gaining a certain amount of respect and trust.

It isn't likely that you will be able to obtain anyone's loyalty so soon, but you must take steps that will make your staff want to develop loyalties. One of the better ways to do this is to have individual meetings with the people you will be working closely or directly with in the future. It is usually best to have these individual meetings before having an initial meeting of the whole staff. First, it will prevent them from making prejudgments about you; second, it will be very flattering to them that you care to meet them privately; third, it will give you a chance to know what each person thinks and what each person does before taking any specific actions on the job. If there is anyone who "should have had the job" instead of you, this is the time to find out who it is, and what he is feeling.

There is no doubt that some people who have been doing their jobs in certain ways will find a threat to their security if they think a new, unknown boss will be going off in a new direction, possibly with people other than themselves. If you do not plan to make any personnel changes, then you should make that known at these early meetings.

How to Learn

A woman executive told us about her first staff meeting with her new people. "I went in on the premise that they knew more about the daily operation and nitty-gritty workings of the department than I did—even though I had been with the company itself for a number of years.

"I asked for reports—oral—on what each of them did. I asked them to bring in their [computer] books so I could see in black and white what each of them had to handle. They were all great and very cooperative. They were on show and they wanted to make a good impression on me.

"I learned from my staff how the budget was formed and what our goals were for the year. My function was to mesh their goals with those of my boss—I was in a sense a decoder.

"How did I get my management training? I didn't. I was put into a room, given a hat and told to go. Now, that's upper management. I did have lower-management training, because this company had compulsory training programs for us. We learned how to communicate, how to motivate our employees and how to develop interpersonal skills."

More conservative companies have these training programs, and things are laid out very clearly. Other fields don't insist on such training because their survival depends on squeezing fast talent, using it up in a certain way and expecting a turnover of personnel. Other companies that depend on long-term projects and maintaining the same personnel over a period of years can't take chances on their own people not knowing exactly how to do things; these are companies that are technically oriented, such as IBM, and they must have people on whom they can depend. They develop people for the long haul. It is to their profit financially to provide such training, because they will reap the benefits.

Weeding the Garden

One golden rule for any new boss is: be careful whom you fire. We knew of one woman who came into a supervisory position at a travel agency and immediately fired a man who had been a special favorite among his co-workers in other departments. The new boss had no particular reason for firing him—it could have been anyone in that spot, he was just the unlucky one. It made no sense and caused ripples of anger throughout the company. Needless to say, the woman had a very uncooperative group after that.

Some companies protect their employees from this sort of thing. Many major corporations have a uniform fair-practices policy that all their companies must abide by. They also provide management training to maintain a uniform style of administration. Although this may clash with the creative needs of some departments, it does provide a protection against capricious decisions to fire employees who have proven themselves. Any new boss should remember that he is not autonomous. He must see himself as a representative of his company, and must take on the duty of expressing loyalty from the company to the people who work for him. They may have known him only a short while, but they have given much to the company before he came on board. If an employee's tenure ends every time there is a change of boss, then there is little reason for that person to give much to the company.

DO: Exercise your prerogatives when they have been given to you. It is expected that you will use the power that has been granted you. But use it wisely.

DON'T assume that because a situation is grim in a company the fault lies with the people who are there. They may have been suffering more than the company. Make sure you know where the problems exist before firing anyone.

Stealing People

When you are setting up a new department of your own, it may be to your benefit to raid other departments for people you have a good feeling about. Be sure that the person you want has a desire to work for you as well. It can be rather sticky accomplishing this, but if both of you have decided it should be so you can find a way to make it happen. For instance, in one company a young woman had been given the go-ahead to form a new department and head it up. She had always had a good relationship with another woman who was the protégée of one of her colleagues—a colleague she had beaten out for the new position, as it turned out. She thought the protégée would be the ideal person to be her second in command.

Her colleague sensed that something was brewing and told her point-blank to keep away from his assistant. Since the young woman had a simultaneous desire to be hired in the new department, she took it on herself to ask for the job. Both women were delighted, and put their heads together to find a polite way to make the change. The young woman approached her boss and calmly told him what she wanted, but emphasized her gratitude toward him and her fear that he would be upset. He took the news politely and kept his feelings in check. Later it became apparent that he felt betrayed, but he retained his dignity and the transition went smoothly. When it comes to a career the choice lies with the person doing the job. You cannot hold yourself back out of gratitude.

Lateral moves within a company are common and should be expected. If beneficial opportunities arise, they should be taken advantage of. It would be foolish not to make the offer when the person you want would probably leave for something else anyway whenever another opportunity arose. Why should both you and the old boss lose out?

DO: Go after the people you need and want.

DON'T hesitate to reestablish good relations with the person whose larder you raided. One way to do this is eventually to compliment him on the great job he did in helping this person get a leg up in the company. Find some way to strengthen your friendship. Don't ignore the fact that his sensibilities have been bruised. Don't get into it right away, but keep an eye toward any future instance when you can reaffirm your goodwill.

Professional Societies

There are many professional societies that serve certain careers. Some of these societies have significant influence on their professions. The American Medical Association is the prime example. Societies have other uses besides power-building. They keep you from becoming too insular in your profession.

Information is always vital to one's survival, and you must keep abreast of changes to keep yourself in a position of power. You should not eliminate any viable avenue of communication. Societies provide such avenues in newsletters, conventions and the like. They keep you current with who is financially healthy and which companies are having problems. For the person wanting to move up, it is always good to know which way is up.

There are also many kinds of networks in the corporate world, which operate as information-exchange centers. Many people set up an informal network of business friends to establish such a channel. It requires some time, but if you feel a lack of such a dependable "news" source in your area you can take steps to set up some sort of group that meets regularly to talk about things—people in a common area of business meeting quasi-socially at lunch, at gyms, at bars to exchange information.

The ancient Romans saw the value of the public baths for this reason, and in some corporate areas health clubs are starting to gain something of the same versatility.

DO: At least consider joining a professional society. If none is around, make time every few weeks to have drinks with someone in your profession, as a way of exchanging information or just maintaining good friendships. Entertaining selected fellow professionals at home is also a good way to keep abreast of things.

DON'T hide.

The Old-Boy Network

The old-boy network is on its way to becoming a museum piece in American business, primarily because the attitude men have of themselves has changed. Also, so many women have come into the executive area that an old-boy network is becoming less and less feasible. Being an all-male thing, it automatically eliminates too many of the people now needed in arriving at the kinds of decisions that were made before. Women can't join men in all locker rooms, although there are places where it is now possible; women certainly can't join men playing squash at the athletic club, or going to a Butt Hutt together, or do any of the so-called "male-bonding" things that made the old-boy network tick. Today's younger executive male doesn't particularly relate to this way of doing business anymore, seeing a clear separation between "office activities" and "social activities." And many younger men aren't geared to cutting women out of the picture anymore.

Some men rebel as much as women do at the stifling attitudes engendered by old-boy networking. Speaking to one of the early rebels against the system—a man in his midthirties now, who had been ousted from his strong position as a whiz kid some eight years ago—we listened to him detail some of the changes.

"Fifteen years ago I had to shave my beard," he noted. "Now, of course, no one even notices it. There's no longer any obligation to get laid or drunk with colleagues at a convention or after having dinner together. Because of the presence of women in business, stag parties can't really be held, and anyway most guys my age want to keep their sex lives private. That old movie *The Apartment*—that kind of thing is over and done with."

There are really no do's and don'ts regarding the old-boy network. Traces of it are still around: a male boss can still go play squash with a younger male executive, lunch afterward, exchanging talk about the activity, and build a professional friendship. But women can do the same thing.

How to Use Gossip

Listen to gossip, don't add to it. Gossip is something of a newsline for the prospective exec to gain an insight into the motivations of his peers and superiors. It's a way to learn who's playing tricks and of what stripe, so that you can protect yourself. People who play tricks generally play them on anyone who seems to be on the way up.

Gossip is the best indicator of what the power configuration is in the company, since no one gossips about unimportant or uninteresting people. It is a thrill to tell on people, in short to tattle on the stars, no matter how minor their magnitude. Don't panic if you never hear anything about yourself: one of the rules of gossip is never to talk about the people who are present.

Gossip always carries the accurate news of who is on the way out. If someone is about to be fired, rest assured that the office grapevine will have it first. It seldom carries the news of who is moving up, for some reason, but it seldom errs about who's on the skids.

Gossip always carries the complaints, the resentments, the bitternesses that pervade the morale of the office people, from workers up to the top execs. Everyone knows about the little battles and big ones that are being conducted. No two executives can have a confrontation behind closed doors without every secretary in the place knowing by lunchtime. No ultimatum is a secret if the exchange was conducted within the premises of the company offices.

It is very easy to learn gossip, since everyone is bustin' to tell what he knows to someone of equal peerage. Just ask, "What's new?" Or if you have an inkling that something may be new, ask, "What's the story with T.R. and Williams?" Someone will know something.

The best way to learn gossip is to be a sympathetic listener in general. Someone who seems to have little real personal interest in an event but who will listen and perhaps advise is the one who gets the info. Sometimes the best way to draw someone out is to say, "I don't want to get involved in talking about this subject, but I think it may affect this project I'm working on." Then proceed to ask for one fact at a time until the person says, "Look, just to keep the record straight, here's what's happening . . ." and he proceeds to dump the whole story on you because you have convinced him you have a valid need to know but don't care to gossip.

It's also a good idea to build up an image as a wise one, someone who always has a good solution to any problem, so that people will come and spill their guts to you whenever they feel scared. If you have developed a reputation as a sort of sage, you will never have to seek gossip—it will seek you.

Another way to get the fire headed in your direction is to be either a good friend or a good enemy of the person being gossiped about. People have a perverse need to tell bad news about friends to other friends, to tell disastrous news about enemies to other enemies, to get a reaction that they can gossip about to others. The thing about gossip is that people like to find their own original tidbits to pass on so that they feel part of the drama. A person who has real clout does not gather information for this purpose. Be a recipient of gossip, but don't ever have any news to pass on. The reason for this is that if you never gossip, people will trust you more and tell you more.

DO: Be discreet. Don't ever appear overly avid for gossip. Do ask for information from your peers. If you have a grapevine terminal for a secretary, it wouldn't hurt to have the kind of relationship that enables you to glean such items from her.

DON'T reveal your knowledge. If, for example, you are in a stall in the rest room and two people are murmuring snatches of information under the delusion that they are alone in there, don't leave until after they do.

You Really Have to Love It

Ah, the things we forget as we become ever more deeply enmeshed in corporate life. The most important one is to keep having fun with it. The folks who eventually top the heap, you'll notice, still have the same kind of exuberance as the bright kid who just started last week. Even the s.o.b.s who top the heap seem to be having the time of their lives doing the corporate thing.

The only real reason to kill yourself over anything is because you love it. If you hate the whole game and get into doing it for the money, and you constantly fight your real feelings, you ought to get off the train. Or change your approach. Corporate life is for those who enjoy it.

CHAPTER **7**

Big Boss, Little Boss

"Ask—and you may or may not receive."

BACK WHEN YOU were fresh on your first job the phrase "upper management" most likely had little meaning for you. If you were smart—and if you've been moving up you *are* smart—you made it your business to separate that amorphous body into distinct characters: people who have different kinds of power, different kinds of personalities. You watched as they wielded the two of them in concert. Now that you are not Down There, you are dealing more directly with these people, and your knowledge about them and their legendary characteristics will come in handy. By the time you have reached this plateau, you should already know the basic approaches to use on each individual who controls your company.

For example, if one of them hates cologne on men, you would

not approach him wearing Macho Brute No. 5. If the female founder of your company can't stand cigarettes, your intelligence might make the leap into assuming she wouldn't like to have you lighting up anything in her presence. If another officer affects a bulldog expression and keeps his hair clipped precisely close to the scalp, you wouldn't want to get him on the subject of nuclear armaments if you happen to be dovish on the issue. You would have made mental notes about the rages and outrages and reputed excesses of the people you must now have meetings with and report directly to.

Diplomacy is now part of your job. You now tread the fine line between polite and cooperative behavior and asserting yourself to get what you want. For example, you would always respect the positions and titles of these upper level executives, even if they have the manners of a warthog—but there are times when you will have to make sure you are heard. Will they respect you for speaking your mind, or will they find it a fatal character flaw? You must know when dealing with your superiors how to mix toughness on a business level with diplomacy in presenting your ideas with impact.

The basic rule here is always to focus your vociferous and strenuous demands on the issues you are talking about; do not let emotion and anger about personalities seep into the debates. People always respect someone who is fighting for something objective—a project—as long as there is no point at which they feel they are being attacked for a lack of perception, intelligence or foresight. Always exhibit an attitude of respect for the fact that these bosses of yours have gotten where they are. It means a lot to them; their egos are almost certainly tied up in their titles—especially if they happen to be mediocre. Give them their due, and fight for your own projects without stepping on toes.

You also must realize and not forget that you are dealing directly with power now. You should have determined how each of these corporate officers utilizes his or her power when you were getting a focus on their personalities. Some people use power as a bludgeon in business. Such people are not interested in subtleties, in niceties, in compliments or favors. They want to deal on a strictly business basis with executives under them.

They like to see people squirm and be embarrassed. They have high standards and expect you to have a reading on how they want things done, and to do things that way. They don't want to be bothered with what they consider to be *your* duties. They just want the results to base their decisions on. In the corporate body you are the stomach which processes the cud so that they can get the milk.

Other powermongers speak softly but carry a big stick. They know that you know they have power and what they'll do if you forget it. For these types the amenities are most important. Such people do appreciate the delicacy of grace, personality, and the elegant trappings of power. They enjoy the royal show, the privileges, and they can be courted by etiquette as well as talent. They like to watch younger executives and select the best.

There are others who are easier to deal with, since you can still let some of your faults out and be indulged. These are the ones who use power actively and in a benevolent way. Such people have a strong sense of justice, and an even stronger sense of economy. They don't like to waste executives in any way. They don't like to fire people who have received a lot of consideration from the company. They'd rather help even a medium-talent executive produce well than get rid of him. They are there for consultation, to dispense advice, to "look into" situations to see how they can help expedite matters. They like having power, the prestige and position, and see themselves as using their power to make the world a better place generally. They believe in excellence and dislike seeing it degraded in their own companies. They help.

It is to your benefit to understand how the individuals with power in your company work, since you are now in the position of having to convince them of things, especially when the stakes are very high indeed. You can wreck your career at this point if you alienate these power people, or you can practically assure yourself of longevity if you convince them you are truly valuable to the company over the long term.

It must be remembered when dealing with the big shots that producing, generating new ideas and making money for the company are what concerns them most. But it would not be realistic to say that no executive has to spend energy stroking the boss's ego. One of my favorite stories is about the executives at the company Christmas banquet who all stood up to hear the telephone greetings from the company president coming long distance from her holiday lodgings on the Côte d'Azur. Their presence at the banquet was mandatory; hers was not.

No matter how benevolent the people at the top may be, or seem to be, no one who wants a career can afford to ignore their egos. Remember, nobody exerts the kind of energy needed to get to the top unless he or she has a very strong ego demand.

Even if you have not yet reached the point where you are dealing directly with higher-management people, you must take many of the same approaches in dealing with your bosses on the way up. You may encounter even more egotistical bosses at the lower levels, since they often have not yet developed the style and security that enable them to deal with their positions. They are still learning, in a sense—and many of them still may be weeded out before they make it to the big time. When dealing with a boss at a lower level, you are in a sense more dependent on his or her goodwill, since this lower-level exec must present many of your ideas to upper management before they can be approved. On the other hand you have the freedom to make your little egotistical mistakes as well, since the game here is less cut-and-dried than when you are dealing with people at the final stages of their careers.

The Boss Is Always Right

When dealing with your superiors, remember that the boss has the support of the officers of the company. His word has more validity than that of the people who work under him, simply because he is in power. This does not mean you don't stand a chance—just that you have to work harder to make yourself credible when you are right and he is wrong.

It is generally the policy of the company to take the word of the boss, even when he exhibits behavior that is obviously and outrageously unfair. This arises from a natural tendency to avoid having to deal with matters of conflict. If the boss is always right, that settles most matters in advance. The other reason for the attitude is that he has been made a boss by the people over him, and if he makes mistakes and bad decisions it reflects on their ability to evaluate him as a worthy administrator.

Whenever a boss is finally terminated, it is almost never because of administrative incompetence. Usually the reason is that he has lost money for the company; or he has placed his own bosses in a compromising or embarrassing position. Everyone who works for him may hate him and think he's a boob, but until someone in a power position decides he is unlikable or unprofitable, he stays.

Be prepared to take some losses as you move up. Some battles may be forfeited without your losing ground. Sometimes it's to your advantage to give in and not fight your boss if it means he will turn around later and back you very strongly on important career matters. Don't get into the fairness of certain situations; do what is expedient to achieve your overall career goals.

Standing Up/Backing Down

When dealing with your immediate boss you must learn how far you can go in your demands and when to shut your great big mouth. Some bosses see their relationship with their best staff people or executives as a constant proving ground. This is indeed a valid way to gauge the commitment. It can start to wear on your nerves, however, when he seems to be testing and baiting for no apparent reason.

Remember, you cannot always gauge your own effect on other people. Perhaps your commitment to your career and to the company is as strong as ever, but you are taking a little mental vacation. Every so often it is acceptable to regroup and collect one's thoughts. During these periods of introspection, your boss may start to get just a little insecure about what's going on in your mind, and start to challenge you. The challenges may take forms that tick you off.

For example, your boss may suddenly start to denigrate your accomplishments. Or he may start trashing on your favorite staff people, saying he doesn't think that person is really as hot on the job as you have led him to believe. Or he may express negative comments about all your staff people. He may not actually be trying to wake you up to your commitment; he may be reacting in an emotional way to your mood. Whatever the stimulus is, you must respond politically, not emotionally.

This does not mean being a Milquetoast. If the boss has pushed you too far you can take several tacks to counter him.

• YOU CAN PULL a Puzzled Over Paranoia response. This is the one where you make a sort of Bette Davis frown while looking up from some important business matter, and express civil surprise that he thinks something is wrong, when you were going along thinking everything was dandy. The reason for your current pensiveness, you can say, is that you have been so preoccupied with some project you are involved in that perhaps you were not your old jovial, joshing self. Then josh jovially.

• YOUR STAFF COMES under attack. Just add a dash of Amazement Over the Attack after making the Puzzled Over Paranoia response. Here you would get a little stuffy and say you don't understand the remarks being made when . . . and here you would tick off all the remarkable achievements of the recent months made by you and/or your staff. Here you can also throw in a few Dismays that he has not been aware of, or has chosen to ignore, these accomplishments. You can then wonder why any of you should bother putting forth your best efforts if they are going to go by the board Ignored.

If this doesn't rattle his confidence and leave him in some disarray, you can turn around, still not conceding his points, and Promise to Try to Do Better in the future. And after that constantly point out the greatness of your achievements as they happen.

If your boss is, or seems to be, serious in his belief that you are losing ground, you can take this tack:

• ITEMIZE THE DAMAGES. Force him to be specific. Ask him to tell you instance by instance where he thinks you have failed. As each one is stated, you should either discredit it with the real facts or give him his due, or ask what he felt you should have done in such and such a case that would have been better. Usually when someone starts itemizing in this way, the faults appear much smaller than when unexpressed and left to sprout in your boss's mind. Stating a fault often lessens its magnitude. You also are forcing him to confront you with them so that you can answer them, and it's a normal human reaction for him to want to avoid a confrontation where he may be proven wrong. Remember during this itemization that you must not overstep into making him look foolish. Stick with the items, and don't attack the boss's ego.

• YOU OWE ME ONE. Here you use the boss's mistake as leverage to get something you want. Don't be a jerk when using this ploy, since you can offend him to the point where he will just reject your demands out of hand. Always approach the boss as if he held all the cards, no matter how strong your position. Don't threaten anything. If he has messed up something you did, and you both know openly that you were right and he was wrong, you can use the situation to request something else. You have credibility: if you were right before, you will probably be right again. And the boss will probably let you go ahead.

Do not infer that the mistake reflects badly on his decision-making abilities. Everyone can be wrong. Refer only to the issues, not to the stupid way he handled things before. Remember here that he actually does hold all the cards, even if it would hurt him in some tangible way if you should decide to leave the company.

The Optimum Time for a Raise

The best time to ask for more money or perks—perquisites—is when things are going right. (We'll discuss perks more later on.) If you are enjoying a success with one of your projects, if some idea you have conceived has borne plenty of fruit, the time to ask for more money or perks is now when everyone is talking about you and congratulating you. Not before and certainly not afterward. Don't try for more money when things are going bad, unless you can convince your company that more money would help you get things going again.

Sometimes when the company is in trouble, or when there has been a wee bit of a scandal, you may be able to make a play for power and money by presenting yourself as the Last Great Hope, or the New Great Hope. Or by threatening to jump ship if you're valuable enough. If they don't want to lose the good execs with the bad, you may be able to parlay for more money and position just because you're clean. Be warned that you must be very clever about using this ploy, since some companies may react the other way: they may be affronted that you should want to abandon ship when the going gets rough.

By getting a real job offer from another company at this time, you may bolster your chances. Take the Virtuous Stance. Go in and say you know how inopportune it is but you've been offered a job that's extremely attractive—not a job you can't refuse. Don't close the doors here. The point is to parlay for stronger position and money at your present place, since they need all the help they can get. If you wait until the crisis is past, you will lose out, since companies operate on expediencies, not on loyalties.

The basic rule to remember during good times and bad is to get your money and your promotions at the times when you are most indispensable, or more desirable. Don't make any statement or threat unless you are prepared to carry it out.

The Ultimatum should be used only when nothing else works. Sometimes you reach a point where you can't live with a situation, and you know it won't be changed. You are weary of dealing with a constantly nettlesome situation, and no matter how many times you have discussed it the boss or the company always returns to the same point. It's a matter of dignity. You must draw a line.

Suppose you have a boss who never goes long without going on a fault-finding tour of your career. You feel it is interfering with your effectiveness as an executive; look for a way to change the situation. Perhaps you have a confrontation about the situation and it changes temporarily. But gradually the old patterns resume. To have spent years at a place and still have to justify your every action is totally unacceptable. You must find a way to permanently change the situation.

Remember: no boss will attempt a real personality change unless you give him a reason to do so. A line must be drawn by taking a drastic action, and that action is the Ultimatum. You are actually saying, "Either I get what I want or I walk."

Many people confuse the Ultimatum with ultimata, but one chance is probably all you'll get. This technique has no effect when it is used on a regular basis. In fact, it may not work the first time, so you really had better be prepared to walk if you don't get what you want. This is a very drastic measure. It is an intense power play between you and your boss, to see who breaks and gives in.

Remember, no one is so indispensable that the company can't say, "So walk, already!" So, keep these things in mind:

• FIRST, DO NOT make ridiculous demands. Try to determine whether the company can meet them without your drastic stance. The Ultimatum is to be used only when all else has failed. One big-shot exec we knew of had been offered the job of heading up a new division in his company, since he'd done such a brilliant job where he was. He wanted—and demanded rather abrasively—to take on the new division and maintain his status as a sort of imprimatur over the other division. It was such an outrageous request that he was fired altogether, even though his termination did hurt the company. But his bosses found his manner inexcusable. If he had instead offered to act as transitional adviser to his successor, he might have ended up with the power he wanted, and the company would have benefited from his expertise in two areas. As it was, the Ultimatum did everyone harm.

• PROVIDE SOME LEEWAY for the company and yourself. Give them breathing space to accept your offer under the guise that no Ultimatum is being offered, if possible. It may be that you are actually saying, "I can't live with this situation—change it or I leave." But this can be camouflaged by presenting a proposal for an alternative situation. If they refuse to compromise, then you can leave. It never does much good to present the Ultimatum in emotional terms, no matter how angry you may be. Emotions always tend to cloud the issues, alienate bosses and make them less inclined to grant the demands. Be professional. Consider writing a long memo stating your position and your demands. You need not express anger—just professional dissatisfaction. Point out that the current situation is untenable because it interferes with your professional effectiveness, not that it gets you angry every time you think of it.

By avoiding the emotional side of the issue, you are enabling them to gracefully concede to you. It is not always necessary to turn such a situation into a triumph for one and a defeat for another. It may deteriorate into such a state, but don't set the stage for it.

• HAVE SOME OFFER lined up if you feel you cannot just drop out of the market. It is best that the company is not apprised of this offer at the outset. It is a stronger bargaining position for you if they think you are prepared to sacrifice all for your demand. If they know you have another offer, it will be seen as a simple ploy for more money with the same situation.

• DON'T GO AWAY mad. If you lose and decide to leave, try to depart on as good terms as possible. Don't storm out casting imprecations left and right. It may not be possible, since some companies will practically escort you to the door. But if you can leave without expressed rancor, it is best to do so. Not necessary, but preferable. Even the most rank situations can be sweetened later on when the air clears and there is again a mutual need. In business the more doors that are left open, the better off you'll be.

• IF YOU STAY: Does one always lose clout if one concedes defeat and still opts to remain in the intolerable situation? It depends on whether it is actually a defeat or a decision to remain in the position which offers you the best opportunities for reaching your goals despite the setback. Perhaps the company will be more impressed with your decision to remain "loyal" even when you don't always get your way. This could give you more clout later on to get what you want, since the company will, in effect, "owe you one." But in some companies this sort of concession will brand you as a pushover. Give careful consideration to your defeats or decisions to stay. Take into account your company's history of treatment of personnel and your own career goals.

• WHEN YOU GET your way, respond gracefully. Don't act as if you scored a victory. Leave them with their egos intact. You won; they know it; pretend that you both came out ahead. And be prepared to perform. Do what you can to make them look better, by thanking them. Remember that concessions to the Ultimatum in business represent a big retreat on the part of your boss or company. Don't push them farther back than they have chosen to go. See that they understand that you view it as a choice on their part, which indeed it is. They could have told you to walk.

Control or Collaborate?

As an executive you must bear in mind that your boss should treat you as a colleague, not a lackey. As you move up in your career, you should demand as much respect as is expected of you. Too many bosses tend not to change their attitudes toward people who move up from lower positions.

The old *Mary Tyler Moore Show* clearly illustrates this. As Mary was promoted to producer from associate producer, she still typed letters, provided coffee for Mr. Grant and in fact did all the things a secretary would do. Of course this was a TV show, but it happens in real life as well.

Sometimes a boss will respect you, or recognize your abilities, but never let you in on that fact. By degrading your self-confidence, he can have the benefit of your abilities without paying for them, so to speak. He has more control over you. It is a common ploy to keep good people from moving around in their careers, from demanding raises and asking for benefits. By keeping your confidence down, they keep you down.

One boss we knew of used this tactic as a common weapon. He had under him several executives, whom he never complimented except in minimal ways. Raises weren't granted until they had been asked for more than once, and there were long delays in between. He never credited any one person but viewed everything as a group effort. All of this subtly imbued them with the idea that they weren't really that good. One day it became clear to one of them that the boss was asking him for advice on how to handle a political situation, and that the boss was in the situation with his superiors. The executive challenged the boss on it and refused to give him the advice. From that point on, the executive demanded what he wanted and got it, and he decided to move on to a better company.

There are three cardinal attitudes that a boss must nurture in the people who work under him: self-respect, dignity and pride in work. If your boss doesn't respect these things, call him on it.

> **DON'T** let your confidence be shaken by a seemingly indifferent or critical boss. Demand an evaluation of your worth from him. Make him acknowledge your expertise.

The Scapegoat-Maker

What can you do if you are stuck with a boss who builds his security on the fleece of others? Many bosses like to make scapegoats to cover their own deficiencies as managers. They sacrifice underexecutives or creative talents as a matter of course, and get away with it long enough to kill off some good careers or to make things difficult at the least. There is little comfort in the fact that they usually get theirs in the end; the end often comes many years after you get yours, and then who cares? It's simply an item for gossip.

There is in fact very little you can do to save yourself if you are selected for sacrifice, since by the time you find out about it the deed is virtually an accomplished fact. Unless you have access to higher-level officers you are pretty much at the mercy of your boss. If you're ousted, get the best possible severance pay you can, and some good references. If your boss shows signs of guilt, take advantage of it. Ask for everything you think you want, including use of the Xerox machine (resumés), and take whatever valuable contacts you can get away with. Don't be shy. If you are a scapegoat, someone owes you a lot.

The thing to avoid is wallowing in anger—which may not be possible, but don't let it swamp you. Also avoid making derogatory statements about the scapegoat-maker. No one else cares that much; it doesn't do a bit of good.

Generally speaking, the scapegoat-maker will be the most enthusiastic booster you'll have if you play it right. He needs to believe he didn't really hurt you, and if you support the fiction he will go out of his way to make amends—elsewhere. The best kind of politician is the one who snatches victory out of the jaws of defeat. If you have been victimized, play for a victory anyway.

DO: Keep records of memos all through as an advance protection against scapegoat-making. Confront the person when you are under attack and make him or her provide some valid reasons for the accusations. If you have already been terminated, it will be too late. If you see something happening, try to find some way to offset it.

DON'T turn into a whiner after the fact. The time of defeat is not the time to go around looking for sob sisters in the company. Maintain the fiction that you are leaving willingly and get what you can in the way of severance pay.

Rolling Over the Boss

There are times when the opportunity arises to roll over your boss and try to take his position. Often the offer is placed directly in your lap, and the only decision you have to make is about taking it or refusing it. The only times one can successfully engineer a takeover without being offered the job first is when there is a true incompetent in the sought-after spot, or when the person is doing something that can spell disaster for the company. Even then you must already have the trust of people higher up, and that often is difficult to obtain without having gone around your boss. There are times when it is possible to replace a boss who is ill or has a personal problem, such as alcoholism, but because of the guilt surrounding the situation it is difficult to line up allies.

If you are going to take over your boss's job without his cooperation and without his knowing it, you must have built a reputation within the company for being his logical successor. If you are engineering the takeover you must be prepared to lose your job if you fail. The best way to roll over a boss is having the job offered to you from the people on top.

The situation may occur like this: Your boss is away from the office, either on vacation or on business. You are called into the office of someone who is his boss, or even a "neutral" higher up. In the latter case you are probably being checked out to make sure you are able to scratch your nose without knocking your glasses halfway across the room. They don't want to pick a wrong one again, you see. This conversation may be rather puzzling to you, unless you have a hint about what's brewing. You may wonder why this Grand Old Man of the company has deigned to call you into his office for coffee and is asking fairly general questions about how your world turns on the third floor.

You soon know whether or not you made enough of an impression on the G.O.M. because your boss's boss calls you into his office that afternoon—they're in a bit of a rush to make a decision, you see—and asks you point-blank whether you think you could run the department if the opportunity arose. What you do then, of course, is strictly your own business. If you have been thinking along those same lines yourself, one hopes you have the good sense to make yourself very available *if* the opportunity arises. This is a good time also to point out where your strengths compare with your boss's weaknesses—not in a disloyal way, of course—and drop a few hints about what you would hope to achieve to correct some of the errors that have cropped up. Unless you know specifically which matters they are dissatisfied with, it is best not to present your unpatented plan to save the company from ruin. This meeting is, after all, still indefinite. Don't seem too eager or keep the meeting going longer than the boss's boss wants it to go. Don't salivate openly.

At this point in your career you must ask yourself whether or not you are ready for the position wavering before you. It may not actually be offered, but you had better know in your mind for sure what you want to do. Give yourself time to think about it. If you are told, "We are firing your boss and we want you to take over," and you're not interested, you should not say No on the spot. The sensible and respectable thing to do is to think about it overnight. They would owe you that much leeway. If you know for sure that you want it, and have been thinking day and night how to get it, you can say that you feel you can and would do a better job for them and you are receptive to the idea of taking the position.

If It's Offered

Unless you are totally unprepared emotionally and practically, I would advise you to give the job a try. You should know after considering it overnight whether or not to accept; you have been working hand in glove with the person being ousted, after all, and the company has a right to expect that you are the person most intimately acquainted with the problems. When mulling it over and having your own doubts, don't forget to consider that the people making the offer usually don't make it lightly. They should have some evaluation of your abilities and it isn't likely they would make the offer if they didn't think you could do it. The other consideration is that the job is not being done at present in any way that pleases them, and since a change will be made anyway, you should give yourself a chance at it.

DO: Remember that you have been working a long enough time to know the job. If you are going to be ready at any point, you are probably ready now. Remember, too, that the company officers have interviewed you and decided you are worthy of the opportunity. If they think you can do the job, they are as likely to be right as to be wrong. Give them a chance to be right.

DON'T remove yourself from the running, if it is at all possible. Unless you are absolutely sure you can't do the job, you should try it. If you refuse, you may, in fact, kill off any future possibilities of moving up in that company. By saying no you are sort of slapping them in the face. It is a rejection, and a way of saying they were wrong in their judgment of you. It's always better to say yes. "Yes" is a word everyone likes. People who have moved up in business have no understanding of anyone who doesn't want to move up. Don't be afraid of the opportunity.

Covering Yourself

The next step may be that the company decides not to fire the boss after all, which is splendid for you if you can keep your mouth shut. This gives you some time to catch up and roll over him later on, since there is an old saying that incompetents can't change, they can only be replaced. If that is the case you should never sit down and have a heart-to-heart with your boss telling him how you saved his job by not taking it. Never mention any of the above to him or to anyone else at the company. "The walls have ears." His boss will not tell him they made you an offer, and neither should you. You have made an important move forward while he was out of town; don't foul it.

If, on the other hand, another person is put in to replace your boss, you will be starting from scratch. Again, there is not any reason to inform this new person that you were considered first for the job. Just offer your full cooperation. But by the time he comes on, you should have had more opportunities to strengthen your contact with the boss's boss, since you probably have had to do some interim bossing. Do not turn down any offer of friendship. Make as many decisions on your own as possible; show how good you will be in the future. If possible, at this time ask about other opportunities in the company.

You may never have another such legitimate chance as this to get to know a higher-up on a professional basis. This may help you should the new boss coming decide to make some staff changes. It may or may not protect you, but it certainly can't hurt to have friends higher up than a new boss.

Don't hang around languishing too long at the company if you weren't offered the job. Unless you can use the sudden notoriety to convince them to create a new position for you—and they will have had to be very impressed with you to do that—you should use the newly minted self-esteem to go get yourself something better somewhere else. If they know you're leaving, they may wake up to trying to keep you. Promises of vague things in the future do not a career make.

DON'T allow yourself to remain as an underling of the new boss. He doesn't know you, doesn't much care about you, and probably will make you prove yourself from scratch. And why should you? If the company valued you enough to tap you for a possible advancement, why should you be moved back two spaces to what amounts to being a new employee? You have proved yourself, you have even handled parts of the boss's job. This is no time to be demoted. Look to up your position with your own company or seek one with another.

Palace Revolts

One of the best things you can do with corporate palace revolts is to stay out of them until you're sure where the chips will fall, and swing your support to the winning party on the eve of his triumph. The best kinds of people to engage in such matters are those who have ice water in their veins. If there is no way you can remain fully neutral, you should run with the foxes and hunt with the hounds as much as possible without committing yourself to either party. This requires an ability to remain as quiet as possible, while visible, since you should never make a statement or comment or verbalization of any kind that would seem to offend any party. If you do make any comments of a definitive kind they should be mildly complimentary to whatever fine qualities either party has.

You should never try to start a palace revolt if you are in a position where you could be fired. You should always bear in mind that people will not like to support anyone in a fight for the truth if it means sticking their necks out and possibly risking their jobs. It does not matter how bad conditions may seem to you; people will put up with the most incredible conditions before they take any action to change them. This is why there are so many police states, so many people who have not had raises for long periods of time, and why people will get up and go to work for someone they hate for years on end without ever making an open statement about it. There is no possibility that people will rally to a cause if it means they might wobble their security.

Even at upper-management levels it is difficult to engineer the ouster of a person who everyone agrees should be ousted. A person in power has the advantage of the incumbent: he is there. That fact alone deters rebellion. Always remember that people see enormous security in the status quo.

DO: Try to work alone as an executive when you are going after something that you want. It makes little sense to try to band together with others at this level. The mentality is all wrong. You will sacrifice your own chances of being advanced later, even if you get some concessions. The management officers do not like this sort of organized revolt. They can respect an individual going after something for himself;

they do not like to have an executive rabble making noises outside the door. If you are intent on building personal power, do not ally yourself with such a band.

DON'T depend on the idealism of the situation to act as some kind of glue for your group. It is easy for your boss to divide and conquer, even if he is in the wrong, since someone in that group will see a chance to make a killing for himself out of a situation created by the group. You will never see such a group gaining any kind of steam, because people are afraid of losing their jobs, and no one will risk losing his job over an ideal.

Shoot Them All at Dawn

Even though it seems like a nasty thing to do, the best course of action—if you take any during this time of palace revolt—is to ally yourself with the power people in the company. Make sure your loyalty to what they consider the reasonable approach is clear. Even though there isn't any real thing that this expression of loyalty does to help the people under attack, you are an ally, and that alone will be worth something. The rewards to be followed should be negotiated now.

If a boss under attack comes and offers you power and position and money to stick with him, accept the offer. If you feel the boss should be toppled, you can work on that later, or rest assured that his position won't be as solid as before. It's best to place yourself in as powerful a position in the succession as you can—even if he places you there himself—to protect your future.

DO: Accept anything beneficial that is ever offered you in business, anytime and anywhere by anyone.

DON'T see yourself as locked into a loyalty to someone who will lose, just because he gave you something useful. Don't moralize about being a traitor to your co-workers. At an executive level there are no finks.

DON'T ally yourself with someone who is being toppled by power people, such as management princes or government agencies. Remember that people under attack from below are always in power positions; people under pressure from above are not. Choose your sides accordingly.

Little Things Mean a Lot

You must have heard of perks—short for perquisites—which, if you look in my dictionary, are defined as compensation in addition to stated income to which one is entitled by virtue of status, position or character. Further definitions state that perks are acquired by one's own exertions—and that's what they are all about. You may also have heard that perks are on the way out, or not as important as they once were. This is not true. If you have clout you can negotiate for perks and they are well worth the negotiation.

First, they do not raise your stated income above a level that places you out of a certain salary range and therefore out of the job market.

Second, many of them are tax deductible, or nontaxable.

Third, they can increase the quality of your life to such an extent that you are living higher than your income after taxes without paying for any of it.

Fourth, they are a statement of your clout in the company.

Perks can take any form you like: interest-free loans; apartments in the city; cars and the gas credit cards that logically should go with them; stock options; free stocks; expense accounts; extra vacation time; use of company due bills at fabulous restaurants, hotels or spas; American Express Gold cards;

clothes; limousine service; haircuts; free medical and dental treatment. You name it. If the company can agree to it, you should try to get it.

Generally, perks are the privilege of those who are stars of the company, those whose efforts and talents have made enough money for the company to warrant these extras. They can also be the bargaining point of people who are not such hotshots but who need more money. In such a case, when the raise is not available the company may be able to provide extra benefits, such as major medical insurance, use of due bills, and limited expense accounts. Perhaps it can be that instead of a raise you can negotiate a vacation at a company-billed hotel with first-class accommodations.

DO: Get all the perks you can negotiate.

DON'T trade real position and advancement for the glamor of perks. Riding first class in a plane is nice, but is it really worth trading off some important thing in your career for? Sometimes companies may offer perks in lieu of advancement, to mollify you. Should you give up the fight because you can stay at the Ritz? Don't think perks mean clout. Clout gets you perks, not the other way around. Always analyze the worth of perks before going for them.

Remember

When dealing with any officer of the company, any boss, any higher-up, remember that their benevolence arises out of the need to do business for the company. It may be that you also become friends with your bosses, but don't lose sight of why you are all at work together. We knew of one executive whose whole basis of success was founded on the fact that the head of the company saw something of himself in the young man. Since they were both somewhat lumpish of mind, the connection was clear to all around. But their connection didn't stop the company head from selling the younger exec's division out from under him when an offer was made that even a lumphead could not refuse.

You should be in business for the sake of a career. You are not there to make friends, make a home, or settle down. If these things also happen, and do not interfere with your career focus, that's okay. Do not make them your career goal, do not let them interfere with it.

Breaking the Mold:

Women Move In

"The brain's the same . . ."

IF WE WERE doing this book five years from now there would not be any reason to have a separate chapter on women in the corporate situation. The major innovation and change in business in the past ten years is the influx of women into key positions at all levels of executive function. It has been awesome. In less than ten years the whole face of business has changed because women have finally moved into administrative and power positions in significant numbers. Everything in these areas has changed accordingly: the etiquette; the interaction between men and women everywhere else; even the way women dress for work.

There are areas of the country where the antifemale attitude is still strong, but it can be said at this writing that women have arrived and there is no turning back. Many people feel that not enough gains have been made, and that many women still have not changed their basic attitudes about being women in business. Others point out that men still resent women and scorn the changes. All this is quite true.

On the other hand there are whole areas of corporate consideration that are dominated by women. Women are running the show at the junior- and middle-executive levels and becoming more visible in higher corporate levels as well. Given the fact that these will have more women employees to promote execs from, the future seems pretty obvious.

There are professional areas where women are still very much discriminated against even though some gains are being made. Even in places where women have been welcome for their talents and given real opportunities as well as proper financial compensation, there is still a lot of rough ground to work out. But it's comforting to know that women's gains have come fairly swiftly since the ascendance of women in business began. Women are making it. Where once they were considered only as consumers, now they are becoming equally important as the sellers.

E.R.A.tionalities

Male chauvinism is alive and well in some parts of the country, and alive but not really all that well in others. Many men who feel chauvinistic in New York, for example, are willing to admit they are wrong and try to put aside their feelings to give women the opportunities they want. In Denver, however, some people wax wroth over the use of the term "Ms." on a letter. There is a great deal of unevenness of attitude on the subject of women in the marketplace.

I was once asked for some advice by a young businessman working in Colorado. He had some valued clients in a female-run company in that area and had developed a good relationship with these women professionally. One day they said they really appreciated his consideration and it was refreshing for them to work with a man who wasn't against the Equal Rights Amendment. He told them he was against the E.R.A. Now, he said, he was worried that he had damaged his standing with them. When I suggested that he should not have made any comment, that he should have agreed that his actions fit his attitudes, he became horrified that anyone, even a valuable client, should think he would be for such a thing.

This dichotomy of attitude is very confusing to many women, not to mention many men. The point here is that even people who have strong feelings about women's rights will still be happy to cooperate if it means financial profit.

Living with Male-Think

I interviewed a young woman, about twenty-eight years old, who was head of her own division in a large corporation. She said she was aware of the problems of being a woman in what was still "a man's world," but she preferred to work alongside the attitudes rather than use up her energies in antagonistic stances on matters that she felt would clear themselves up over the years anyway.

"Women have to stop and take a look at the changes that have been made, and to accept the fact that there have been important changes in practice," she said. "Yes, there is an old-boy network, and younger men have the advantage of being able to communicate in certain ways with older male executives, but I can't sit around being distressed by it. I make my way in my own way and it hasn't held me back so far. A lot of that old-boy thing will die of natural causes as women make more and more gains, and then there will probably be an old-girl network. Good Lord, I'll probably be one of the old girls!"

This pragmatic approach makes eminently good sense, spoken by a woman who sees the openings rather than the blocks to her career, who realizes that everyone has some tough nut to crack in business. Men may have an advantage over women in many cases because of being men, but they can't hold on unless they have the talent to compete with the women. Although the old-boy network gives certain men a certain edge, it also puts pressures on them to be "on" all the time in situations that do not directly pertain to business. Not all men these days think along the same lines as the old boys, either, so the pressure of having to act in a preordained way can be as deleterious as being excluded altogether.

DO: Keep your priorities in focus. Take advantage of the opportunities that exist and create new opportunities out of them. Each time there is an opening, it clears the way for another step forward. Once you prove yourself at one job it is easier to move up from there. The change has been made and the atmosphere is then geared to more changes relating to you. If you think in terms of being seen as someone who is a viable executive, then the thinking will be set in the minds of others as well.

DON'T waste time boiling in anger over changes that haven't been made. Part of having a career is having fun with it. Focus your energies toward achievements and enjoying your career.

Communicating with Men

This isn't easy, and no one should pretend that it is. There are, however, two sides to be dealt with whenever there is a major change in any area. Compromises are required on both sides. Yes, there have been frustrating and infuriating inequities. The attitudes of many men about women in business are maddening. The point is to accept the fact that even when dealing with such intractable people as male chauvinist pigs—and women who think they're just A-okay—you must take the approach that works, not necessarily the approach that is righteous. If you must work around such people to win in the final heat, then do it. You aren't accommodating to their attitude, you are just taking effective ways to eliminate it.

The stand has been taken. The feminist pioneers have cracked the foundations and they are crumbling. It's time now to take other stands. You have a job in business, now you can move ahead through political awareness and talent. Why waste your time refusing to budge because someone is baiting you about being a woman? Ignore this person and move past him.

You can take the other approach of sitting down and discussing the matter with him. If you have a man who works with you or for you—or against you—don't get into a war of nerves with him. Admit that there is a problem, also that it may be a problem of man versus woman, and take the initiative. Ask him to sit down and exchange formal gripes with you for the purpose of arriving at a workable relationship in the office. If you take such a professional tack, there is no way he can refuse without damaging his own standing. If your differences come out of nervousness—say, his not knowing how to deal with a woman on a professional basis—give him some direct pointers on how you would like to be treated.

If he holds the door for you or lights your cigarette, or makes remarks starting with "Women always . . . ," tell him exactly what you feel he should do instead. Don't just complain without giving a positive direction. Many men want to relate to women as co-workers but have had no previous experience. Give them help. It will benefit you and give you a real boost in their way of viewing you professionally. No one can ignore a truly intelligent approach to a business problem—no one can afford to.

Business is communication. If you prefer to seethe and rant when a solution that would end the problem is available, then you are holding yourself back. Never let your ego or emotions get the upper hand in a man-versus-woman situation in the office. If you come up with a solution, you will win.

DO: Remember that positive communication will get better results than flaring up over things that have had too little time to be governed by established patterns. Help set the standards by vocalizing your wishes.

DON'T turn on someone like a puff adder just because he tried to do something out of a genuine sense of politeness.

Chitchat

Information within a corporate structure is usually passed in conversation. It is often difficult for a woman to gain access to this if the company is male-dominated, since the men are not likely to invite "the new girl" along to the pub, where they will automatically start talking about who's doing what in which department, which openings are coming up that may be available for the right person. In effect a woman in such a situation is frozen out unless she has a good buddy in the form of a man who also gets together with her and passes along the scuttlebutt.

That is, in fact, one good way to gain access to this informational network: make a good buddy of a man who likes you. The formal and informal networks are the key to being with it in your company. You must be aware of what is happening. In some companies women have little problem learning useful gossip, that concerning staff changes and company policy and opportunities; in others the male dominance may work against women.

"I had to charm and force my way into meetings," one woman who worked in a highly macho company said. "They would have meetings that were not posted and I wasn't told about them—and I was a manager. I had to keep my ears open all the time, and go and ask, 'Is this meeting for me too? Why not?' Of course I was just being cut out because I was a woman, even though I had the same job. They thought of their meetings as male things. Eventually they came around when they saw I was made of the same corporate stuff—and that they didn't have to watch their mouths when I was there."

Make friends with men in such businesses. They are only following patterns that can be broken. One woman who worked in a highly technical field and who had made it to department head over an all-male staff told us this story:

"We were all out on a boat—no spouses were with us. The boss came up from below and said, 'We need some coffee,' and everyone on the boat—including the men who worked under me—turned to me as the woman present. I was expected to make the coffee. I just said, 'I'll have cream and sugar,' and someone else had to do it. Good thing. I don't know how to make coffee. My husband does it at home."

Charm and wit are big boosts for the woman who must deal with these serious structures of male-oriented thinking. There are many ways to make changes, but the quickest and most enduring way is to make men want to change; to make men want women working side by side with them. It helps get you where you want to be without creating more obstacles along the way.

DO: Make friends with the guys in the company. Show that you don't expect any special treatment. If you are in a male-dominated area, go along with the prevailing chitchat there. Make friends, ask for information, ask ask ask.

DON'T be a bitch. Men like people who can take a ribbing, and they usually express affection through joking put-downs or good-natured barbs. They like it when it can be returned without rancor. Some men do express themselves in the straightforward way that women do, and this may be easier for you to handle. If you are in a female-dominated office, remember that the men there may be experiencing the same thing that women do with a lot of men. Try to be understanding when there seems to be no communication along the conversational line. Women and men do tend to speak in different languages.

Paternalism

This has been a common complaint among women who work for older men. The man has had no experience in his life that would enable him to relate to a woman other than as to a wife, a daughter, a niece or a secretary. So he adapts one of these social approaches to women in business. If you are young enough to be a niece or a daughter and you aren't a secretary—well, you can guess the rest.

Some women do not see this as a particularly negative response. "I see men taking the same tack with younger men," one high-placed woman exec told me. "Why shouldn't he do the same with women just starting out? I don't see it as degrading."

"I don't see it as degrading, either," says another young woman, "But I do see it as embarrassing. I am an adult, and it kind of embarrasses me to get into this play-game with someone I work with. I might do it with my husband as a courting game, but in the office I feel kind of silly."

There are two ways to approach this. Realize that the man is probably well disposed toward women in business, and kind of coach him through. He is probably very embarrassed about his lack of ability to know how to deal with the new situation and is coping the only way he knows how. Management training seminars should include some retraining for these good men, but often don't—or the men don't take advantage of them.

You can either go along with it, while subtly leading him into more professional ways of acting toward you, or if he is this kind of person, ask if you can discuss it with him. I personally feel that the first way is better, since the man in question is probably doing something he feels is helpful to you. By establishing a positive relationship and taking the time to rechannel, you will get better results in the long run without a negative block.

DO: Use every advantage you have when trying to move ahead. If a boss is well disposed toward seeing you advance, but the only way he can express himself is through patterns he knows, don't reject his help. Make friends, and when he is more comfortable with your working together you can gently suggest changes if you still feel they are necessary.

DON'T get locked into programmed reactions. Always look for the intent behind the action.

Older people have spent years successfully working with certain behavior patterns. Don't expect them to drop them like an old topcoat just because there has been a wave of change. Look to the future. Younger male executives are already responding and acting differently from their predecessors.

Women and Women

Do older successful women stand in the way of younger ones? Some do; others help them get ahead. It is an individual thing. Many established women feel that since they had to hack out such a rough path through the corporate jungle all women should go through the same trial by fire. This is nonsense, of course. You can't help it if you were born in 1950 instead of in 1928.

If a woman is working against you because you're a woman and she's a bitter old prune, the best tack to take is to prove your mettle to her. Some people change when they see themselves in someone else. If she is making things rough for you, don't complain, succeed. Don't let her break you. There is always a way to find how to do something in business. If you have the kind of ingenuity to succeed in spite of obstacles, you are bound to roll over her or gain her help and respect.

DO: Try to build a network of loyal business friends among women, but also do the same thing with men. Try to help younger women get into the business, but don't allow yourself to be used badly just because the two of you are of the same sex.

DON'T waste time on people who are standing in your way, male or female. If you are getting flack, focus your energies into another direction, make your own contacts, build your own experience through getting help elsewhere, or find it in yourself. Don't be held back by someone who is bitter or envious.

The Big Chill

We were told once about a department which had five people at the same junior-executive level, all competing for the same advancements. Four of them were women and one was a man. The man, it so happened, was not as hot a talent as the women, yet he was getting the favors from the boss. "We didn't like it," said one of the women, "but because he was a man he could go to the health club with the boss and in general could pal around with him. He was the only one the boss felt really comfortable with.

"Then we found he was using his advantage to make us look bad, to take credit for some things that we came up with as group ideas and projects. So we ganged up on him and shut him out. If he was going to take credit, we decided to let him come up with the ideas. We just didn't say anything at meetings or when he was present. He started getting scared, so finally we had it out with him and brought him into line. The boss started getting a clearer picture, and all got a more even distribution of credit and favor."

This idea of freezing out a snipe like that is always a good one. It is in fact about the only way to handle a situation short of making complaints that may be taken as jealousies or ganging up on a favorite. At this early level the smart ones should always try to cooperate against the evil ones, so to speak. Things are too important at this point to let yourselves be divided by egotistic matters. There is a long road ahead and you should be able to travel it equally without letting someone sidetrack you.

DO: This is where establishing friendships professionally helps—networking again. Do force low-talent mavericks to prove themselves, to work superhard if they are trying to discredit you. Do freeze them out. Do make them look awkward and inept whenever necessary. Let them play it straight or take the chance of drowning—on their own.

DON'T help a snake. Everyone needs backup and friends in a corporate situation, above and below. No one can be held up by someone from above if there's no support for him below. Eventually the rope breaks and it's bye-bye, Buck Rogers.

Should You Have Sex?

Whenever you have men and women in the same enclosed area you have the question arising: Should I make a pass? The answer in the office is usually: No, I shouldn't. Most people go with that sensible decision and either go on to fantasize about someone on the bus or at the lunch counter or looking in the window at Bergdorf Goodman. Very often, however, you have these slaves to passion who can't control themselves and go ahead to the mattresses.

Let us say, first of all, that people are going to have sex. In our culture we haven't provided many viable places for people to come into contact with safe partners on a casual basis. The office is one of the few sites for such meetings, and, as you would expect, it happens, and it happens perhaps more often than can be polled. It is not a good idea to allow yourself to be drawn into such an arrangement on a one-shot basis and certainly not into a long-term affair. This is not to say that you should avoid the opportunity to date people you are truly interested in, although these aboveboard socially acceptable dates should not take place in the same department if it can be avoided. A totally sexual arrangement is not good office politics.

I have never heard of any such affair, except one—and that one would have become a marriage if not for a very unusual state of affairs—where someone didn't lose his or her job as a direct result of the affair. Sometimes the loser was not even one of the two lovers, but someone who was adversely affected because the relationship came to affect the working place. Even if the sexual affair turns into a permanent, loving relationship, it still brings havoc to the office. The only people who can have these affairs are people who are so mature that they can skillfully separate the office from the home; people who do not have jobs that are important enough to affect others—and even then they must maintain strict discretion in the office; and people who are physically separate from each other in the office itself.

If you are young and attractive you must be careful not to fall victim to an affair. If you want to move up in a professional way, you should be alert to the fact that as a young executive you have enough to handle just learning administrative skills; to take on the complexities of sexual yearnings and burnings on top of that will only hinder your progress. Have your tacky little flings with people you meet socially, or forgo them, but don't play with fiery co-workers.

DO: Let yourself get to know someone on a professional level. If you feel an attraction, let it rest unless it turns into a valid emotional sharing that you may want to explore on a serious level. Do keep the whole thing out of the office —even to talking about it with each other or co-workers. If you do find that love has found the two of you in adjacent offices, make your plans accordingly as far as announcing it. If you are colleagues and will not be competing with each other professionally, and one will not become a boss over the other, then you should be able to retain your jobs. If not, one of you should transfer.

DON'T give in to the forbidden-fruit syndrome. Very often the wanting is based on the fact that you shouldn't have; this is a basic courtship thing that springs from a biological pattern. That's why birdies peck each other on the head for three days before they decide on the number of eggs. Also remember that the having very often is not as thrilling as the wanting.

The Use of Wiles

Most women today are of a different set of mind than those who once used "women's wiles" to get ahead. There is no doubt that many women still sleep their way into certain positions. This may be because they consider it a shortcut, or because they do not trust in their own talents to get them there, or because they're in a real hurry. Many women who take this route are often talented, but there are obvious flaws in their approaches. It is the same with anyone who feels the need to use sexual or politically underhanded methods to gain power and position. If they could do it on merit alone they'd be better at the job; since the merit doesn't match the political or sexual ability, they go for it anyway. It always shows, even when the overall effect seems successful.

One problem as some women see it is that affirmative action has become a weakened tool in America. The government has clearly stopped taking any kind of protective action for minority groups, so many women feel that they must take drastic steps on an individual basis. The woman who is secure in her talent and business ability is a lucky person. She knows she won't be affected by the ups and downs of fate, because she's in control of her own destiny. But even women who are sure of themselves may want to rely on mentors, or use paternalism, to facilitate getting what they want on an executive level.

There is little use in sitting in judgment here about such matters. It must always be remembered by anyone who takes what might be termed the low road that you'd better have the talent to back up your performance once you're in power. You'll need it. Or you'd better keep your political acumen or sexual acumen in top form. Something has to keep you in power once you've gotten there.

DO: Press whatever advantages you have. Younger men who are superjocks aren't afraid to use that glamor to gain advantages over scholarly types. It's the same syndrome. If you have a glamorous image of any sort, and the people in power want to give you things because of it—or at least listen to you more carefully—this is a distinct political advantage. This is a sort of power. If you have it, use it.

DON'T rely totally on the wiles or the glamor. Use the advantage to display your more business-like talents. Once the people in power are listening, tell them what you want them to hear. Remember, too, that many of the beauties—male or female—are seldom taken seriously as having brains. People like to give them opportunities anyway, as a way of vicariously sharing in the gorgeousness. If you have this advantage/disadvantage, remember you will have to work a touch harder to overcome the preconception that beautiful people can't be smart. Use the first part to get a chance to prove the second part.

Establishing the Image

A very smart woman who is having a very good career in business as a writer and consultant told me that at present there is no identifiable image of a businesswoman. "There is a definite image for men, however," she noted. "If a man—or a male of any age—walks into a reception area, the receptionist knows immediately why he's there: she knows whether he's going to deliver a package or going to want to speak to an executive. When I walk in, even dressed in my own version of what the well-dressed businesswoman wears, I get this suspicious scrutiny, like 'What do you want?' I think we women have to arrive at that immediately identifiable image so we don't have to explain ourselves."

Women have never really had a defined way of dressing for the office. As little as twelve years ago women wore summer dresses, with much, shall we say, collarbone on view. Bare arms were also commonplace among the distaff members of the working staff. The rare woman who had achieved status in the executive hierarchy generally wore a mature version of the preppie look, or something severe much like Barbara Stanwyck clawing her way to the top.

The woman today who vies for a place in the corporate sun does not show much more skin than the males she is striving to compete with. Today's woman has found it to her advantage to cover up to the neck. Smart move. Some women have gone overboard by adapting blue serge pinstripe outfits replete with modified neckties and shirt collars. Dumb move.

Point number one: There is no need to surrender your femininity to make it to the top. A woman can dress in a businesslike way without compromising female choices. Look at it this way: The standard male business suit highlights and emphasizes the preferred male physique—broad shoulders, tapered waist. A man in a suit makes a good impression on other males and is attractive to women as well. He looks good as a man. This is the point of image-building. Now, if a woman wants to imitate this ploy, she should avoid clothes that make men look good and aim for clothes that make women look good. This does not mean that she should dress in sexually provocative clothes. Men do not wear tank tops and gym shorts to the office, after all. The woman should adopt a conservative feminine look that makes her look serious about her work while making her look good.

One of the best-turned-out businesswomen I ever saw was a young lawyer with a reputable firm in New York. She tended toward charcoal grays, muted patterns, but with a feminine flair that indicated good taste and self-respect. The clothes were cut well, providing a lot of room for movement—full skirt and an ample tailored short jacket. The blouse was a woman's blouse, not an adapted man's shirt. Her makeup was monotoned, to complement her dark-blond hair, which she wore in a style that would adapt easily to sport, business or the theater. She thought her clothes were boring. "I open the closet and see this lineup of sameness on the hangers for work," she said. What she could not see was the striking impression she made as a businesswoman in the setting of her company's elegant offices. She fit in. She looked good. You wanted to look at her as an attractive woman, but you wanted also to hear what she had to tell you about your legal problems. The look worked.

Another woman I met at a seminar impressed me with her intelligence and focus on her career, but she dressed poorly. She wore a brown leather jacket, a bold colorful plaid skirt and a textured blouse. Her makeup and hair were entirely too mauve for the office, and each piece of clothing was at odds with the others. She was bright, but she had been taking the rainbow route. There would have been nothing wrong with the way she dressed if she were going to an afternoon event, but it did not establish a good image for the businesswoman.

DO: Establish a personal style of dressing, expressing your business image through your clothes, while staying within the parameters of proper corporate attire. Small items, such as a favorite item of jewelry—or no jewelry at all ever—can become part of your mystique. Don't do it in an artificial way, but utilize some particular way of dressing or accessorizing that makes you feel good, and go with it. Be sure that the chosen style won't become dated over the years, or later on you'll look like a preserved page of *W*. Pick something that can be considered a future classic.

DON'T dress like a man. It seldom looks good on a woman, unless you're a model or an actress doing a takeoff on men. For the office adapt clothes that enhance your feminine proportions in a conservative way. A business suit for a woman is a smart idea, but it must be designed on her proportions, not on a man's.

Dressing Down

One very successful woman I know prefers to dress in tee shirt and jeans. It works for her because of the kind of person she is, but it won't work for everyone. She can get away with it only because she has that kind of image, and she's bright enough to carry it off. These days, with the more conservative set of young people in business, it would not be advisable to adopt this kind of dressing.

I met a young woman, around nineteen or so, who was working for a major newspaper in the Midwest. She showed up for an interview wearing a gingham blouse and a jumper that was sort of an adaptation of a farmer's overalls. She also had a heavy scattering of freckles, so the general impression was that she was a country girl here to take notes for *Henpickin' Press*. She asked me what advice I would give her to get ahead in her career, and I suggested she upgrade her image. She seemed offended or puzzled, so I softened it and said if she wanted to be taken seriously she should wear more businesslike clothes. The frown deepened. I then said she should try for jackets and skirts, and the frown became a smirk of annoyance. I also said she should concentrate on being a good reporter, and then I remembered some of the questions she had asked. I figured she should aim for a career as a milkmaid somewhere and said, "Well, you'll probably grow into your own niche," and let it go at that.

You cannot hang on to certain attitudes if you want to make it as a serious career person in business. You cannot hang on to childish images that work in a certain collegiate atmosphere. When you get into the big people's world, you have to make a change into being an adult yourself. If you are truly serious about your career, don't get hung up on rebelliousness. It is a waste of time, and no one but you will pay for it. To hang on to a way of dressing that is inappropriate is probably the most absurd way to waste your early years in business. There are so many better ways to channel your energy to your own advantage. If you resent the ways of the corporate world, then why are you there? The best way to win in business is to beat them at their own game.

We spoke to a retired woman who has had a successful career as an executive. She feels there are some general guidelines that women can follow about how to dress appropriately for business.

Starting from the top, she feels that a corporate head, a woman who has founded her own business, or someone right up there with the big shots, can wear "a very expensive dress, or a jacket-and-skirt combination with a beautiful feminine blouse. Simple elegant jewelry in keeping with her income, as well."

Lower down the ladder, she feels that women in upper- and middle-executive positions should be more uniform and rigid about their choices. "Suits, definitely, but not those masculine horrors with the little ties. Every time I see those, I want to rip them off their necks—or strangle them with them." Don't sacrifice femininity for men's suitings. Allow some style and cut to take the place of color and spectacle. Concentrate on female blouses and neckware rather than male ties.

Secretaries should aim for dresses, not slacks, unless they work in places where fast-fashion style is part of the game, such as in record companies. Makeup should be subdued in the office for all women, although secretaries and receptionists, being younger in general, can get away with more color combining.

Sweaters can work for some careers, but not often. High-impact perfumes are not advisable. Makeup should be there to help, not to dazzle. This is true at all levels. Jewelry should be conservative and tasteful and simple. Hair should be to your taste without getting outrageous.

DO: Leave yourself open to changing your way of dressing as you get older. What looked great on a woman of twenty-two will look kind of funny on a woman of thirty-five. Part of supporting a business image is knowing what looks good at certain stages of maturity. Your look should always reflect your position, your current way of thinking, your self-assurance and your acceptance of the natural progression of your womanhood.

DON'T groom in public. Too many women develop habits of lipsticking, brushing and powdering in public. It does not look good when a grown woman suddenly pulls out her compact in the office or at a luncheon table during a break. They call certain rooms "women's lounges" for a reason. Find out why. Men should not shave at their desks; women should not apply eyeliner there, either.

Everyone Out of the Pool

Although many great entrepreneurs rose up out of the mailroom, not many people think of a secretarial pool as a nurturing place for future corporate talent. Part of this is self-fulfilling prophecy: no one expects secretaries in the pool to mature into ambitious businesswomen, and neither do they—so they don't, usually. The same basic rules for advancement apply here as they do anywhere else in business. If you make a real decision to move ahead, get special training to help you climb, and keep your eyes and ears peeled for opportunity, you'll get there.

One successful black woman told us that it takes a lot of sacrifice and patience for several years, but if you want to move into executive levels anyone can do it. "I made my decision when I was working in this gossip-ridden secretarial pool," she says. "I started by upgrading my skills and getting my B.A. Every time I heard about an opening I'd apply for it. Eventually I got the idea: they were putting up these notices because legally they had to, but the positions were always filled. So I got the bright idea to take a day off and I went to every government agency office in town with my resumé and applied for jobs. I knew something had to break and it did. From there I jockeyed around from a better position until I got what I wanted—an executive secretary's job."

It doesn't do any good to wait until something opens or doesn't open if you want out of the pool. You have to make yourself noticed in a positive way. As in any business, you have to see what the "buying public" wants and give it to them. In the case of secretaries, what they want are top skills, and personalities that can work with other people.

Some mistakes that pool secretaries make are based on the idea that nobody notices them, so they don't take special pains to put forward a professional business image. This is wrong. Nobody is truly invisible in a business office. If people do not notice you, it's because you are presenting such a down image that they prefer to ignore you.

Specifically, these are common errors made in the pool:

• NOT DRESSING THE BUSINESS PART. Yes, there are laws that say a company may not discriminate against you because you like to dress a certain way, but like so many laws of their kind they miss the point and protect no one. Grow up. As one executive secretary said, "Most pool secretaries *dress* like they're in a pool." They wear blue jeans, pants outfits that are great for doing a Gloria Vanderbilt commercial, but that do nothing to strengthen one's business image. Tight pants don't go with a corporate setting.

• TOO MUCH MAKEUP. You should never go to work looking like a clown unless you happen to work for Barnum & Bailey. Too many young women in business, especially in secretarial pools, don't know when to stop with the color brushes. If you want to wear spectacular makeup, wear it at the disco, at parties, somewhere else, not the office. You aren't here to compete with lights or look simply fab. You're here to work and to look presentable while you work. In the office, concerning makeup and personal décor, remember, less is more.

• TERMINOLOGY. This area concerns the young woman's mouth and what comes out of it. Vulgar talk, the use of common four-letter words, shrillness of voice and machine-gun chatter all work against you. Constant gossip, complaining about everything and everyone, casualness of attitude and a lack of awareness about how you come off will only stand in your own way. Basic rules of the pool can be summed up this way: If you can't say something nice about someone, don't say it at all. If you talk that way to your girlfriends or your family, chances are you should find some other way to talk to your co-workers and bosses. If you don't know exactly what formalized business attitudes consist of, get some professional training right away. Ask your bosses to tell you if they think you should improve your act in any way, and don't get mad when they tell you the truth.

• DON'T CHEW GUM. Or don't chew gum when you're talking to an executive, even if you're on a friendly basis.

• DON'T GROOM AT YOUR DESK. Many women in business are not aware of the fact that most men are offended by having to watch them comb, style and make up in full view of the office. If you feel you have to do this, then it's time to get yourself an office look that doesn't require fixing in public. This lack of sensitivity to other people's feelings will work against you in the long run.

• MESSY DESKS. It may seem like an impossible task for a hassled secretary to have to keep her desk organized, but the fact is you must. If you were an executive secretary you'd have to keep two desks and offices organized. If you don't think you can take on the extra load without cracking, then you certainly could not take the pressure of working in a higher position. Executives don't want to know how their secretaries manage to do so much, they only want secretaries who can do so much and more. The one thing they notice first is how messy your desk is, and they judge that.

The secretary who stands out in a positive way is the one who will move up, says our favorite executive secretary.

DO: Shape yourself up into a highly disciplined professional. Once you do, it will impart to you an aura that people will read and respond to immediately. This will boost you up the ladder.

DON'T whine to yourself about things not coming your way. Usually the block to anyone's success lies in her own attitude toward herself. If you think you won't get something, then you won't. If one woman can make it in the corporate world, so can hundreds, thousands. It all depends on changing the way you think as much as the way men think.

Where the Goals Are

For a young secretary with business aspirations it is important to learn what is available to her, and what kind of education is required from her. Even though secretarial salaries seldom keep pace with either the work required or the educational background brought to the job, the preference at the moment is for secretaries who have completed four years of college as well as secretarial training. It is by no means necessary that a secretary have a B.A., but it is certainly a big help in applying for other jobs, or in moving out of secretarial jobs and into junior-executive positions.

It is an interesting point that many administrative jobs these days are more or less secretarial although called by other names. The difference is that the salaries are more open-ended and advancement is not limited. It may be useful to a secretary to look closely and inquire about any kind of assistant-type position when looking for a way up.

A secretary who wants to forge ahead should collect information when deciding on a goal for the future. If you want to maintain the secretarial career, then make inquiries within your own company about advancement opportunities. Keep your resumé up to date, and read the want ads regularly. Send out your resumé when it seems that certain openings may be right for you. If there is a particular corporation you want to work for, or a certain area you want to be connected with, such as publishing or advertising, then take the initiative and make an appointment for an interview with their personnel department on your day off. Such matters can be kept confidential if you choose. Just ask that nobody contact your current boss without asking you first.

Do not be afraid to ask people you know, even at the executive level, and who are well disposed to you, to give you advice, or to keep you in mind if they know or hear of anything that may fit in with what you are looking for. But try to have some clear idea of the area you want to get into. Don't be afraid to sit down with yourself and make this decision. Then don't be shy about stating your goals to whomever you seek help from. Seventy-five percent of getting ahead is having the guts to go for something. Don't be afraid to get a job interview. You can decide later whether or not to take the job if it's offered. Indecisiveness about trying in the first place is the biggest career killer. You can never know if you want a particular job until you have a real picture of it.

Many people feel that getting used to interviews is a big help in finally getting the job you want. This is not really true. If you are actually looking for a job and know what you want, and are scared of the prospect, then interviews may help you relax. The truth is that if you are right for a certain job and a certain boss, you will shine through a bad interview. Sometimes a little nervousness is what you need to push you into giving your best shot at the interview. If you are too relaxed, too casual, you may not have the right energy to come across in the right way.

Last Word

Each time some new event happens in the business world a whole set of patterns and attitudes becomes suddenly obsolete. It may take time for this obsolescence to be felt widespread, but, as in Donne's poem, when a bell rings it rings for everyone. Women represent the biggest unreversible change in business, despite the fact that many people stubbornly cling to outmoded resentments against the fact. We live in a society where people who want things cannot be denied them, no matter how much resistance is put up to maintain a tired status quo.

The best executives are the ones who can recognize valid changes, decipher them from passing fads, and plan accordingly. The basic interactions in business don't change much, but the kinds of people acting out the games do. The enlightened executive looks to the past to review the need for change, to the present to implement ideas for change, and to the future to ensure movement through change. To try to hold the line anywhere is a waste of energies. The very nature of society is progressive. We cannot lock ourselves into stagnant attitudes that serve only a few people.

Index